KS2 English Spelling

Targeted SATs Practice Workbook

SATs Essentials
For the 2019 Tests

Year 6
Ages 10-11

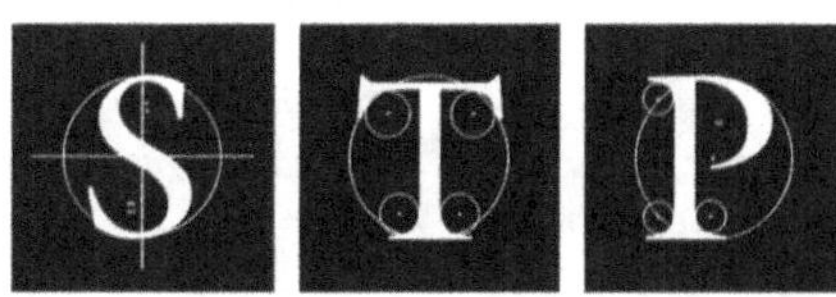

Published by STP Books
An imprint of Swot Tots Publishing Ltd
Kemp House
152-160 City Road
London EC1V 2NX

www.swottotspublishing.com

Text, design, and layout © Swot Tots Publishing Ltd

First published 2017 by Swot Tots Publishing Ltd
This edition published 2018 by STP Books

STP Books have asserted their moral right under the Copyright, Designs and Patents Act, 1988, to be identified as the author of this work.

All rights reserved. Without limiting the rights under copyright reserved above, no part of this publication may be reproduced, stored in a retrieval system, or transmitted in any form or by any means electronic, mechanical, photocopying, printing, recording, or otherwise without either the prior permission of the publishers or a licence permitting restricted copying in the United Kingdom issued by the Copyright Licensing Agency Limited, Barnard's Inn, 86 Fetter Lane, London, EC4A 1EN.

Typeset, cover design, and inside concept design by Swot Tots Publishing Ltd.

British Library Cataloguing in Publication Data. A catalogue record for this book is available from the British Library.

ISBN-978-1-912956-04-3

CONTENTS

For each of the following, underline the one correct spelling from the choices given in brackets.

Example: **The bird chirped (merryly merrily merilly merrilly) in the summer sun.**
The bird chirped (merryly <u>merrily</u> merilly merrilly) in the summer sun.

1. "I think I'll go out (tomorrow tommorrow tommorow tomorow)," said Jim.

2. 'Ali Baba and the (Fourty Fouty Forty Fourtie) Thieves' is a well-loved story.

3. Shaun always (criticises critticises critecises critiscises) everything.

4. The (identite identity identaty identtity) of the winner is not yet known.

5. I love the (variaty varyty varriety variety) of fresh fruit at the local market.

6. The parcel will (probably probibly probbably probabley) arrive after Christmas.

7. Elias looked very (awkuard awkwad awkward awkould) in his new suit.

8. The toilet has been (occuppied occupied ocuppied occupyed) for ages!

9. Scientists are (developing developping develloping developing) a cure for this.

10. The man's face looked very (familyer femilyer familar familiar).

11. Omar raised a (relavant relivent relevant rellevant) point during the discussion.

12. Despite being an (amatuer amateur amator amature), Lucy is a talented singer.

13. John was being (harassed harrassed herassed herrassed) by a persistent salesperson.

14. There has been a (defanite deffinite definite deffinnite) change in the weather.

15. We can't wait for the (twefth twelth twelf twelfth) season of our favourite TV show.

16. Last (Wensday Wendnesday Wednesday Wendsday), we went to the cinema.

17. I have (attached attatched attacthed attacht) the document to this email.

18. The island has been struck by a (categry category categry catigory) 6 hurricane.

19. I walked into the end of the bed and (brused bruised brewsed briused) my thigh.

20. They had a (wunderful wanderful wonderfull wonderful) time with their cousins.

25 words are listed below. However, 10 of them are spelt incorrectly. Find the 10 incorrectly spelt words and write their correct spellings in the spaces provided.

accident	occassion	cemetery	parliment	recognise
dictionery	sincere	determined	explaination	signature
queue	embarass	programe	community	compitition
guarantee	vehicle	physical	corespond	eight
nieghbour	accompany	secretry	yacht	available

21. ________________________________   26. ________________________________

22. ________________________________   27. ________________________________

23. ________________________________   28. ________________________________

24. ________________________________   29. ________________________________

25. ________________________________   30. ________________________________

In each of the following, show whether the given word is spelt correctly or incorrectly. If the word is incorrectly spelt, write the correct spelling in the space provided.

**Examples:**   *chair*   ☑   ________

               saveing   ☒   _saving_

31. neccessary   ☐   ________________________________

32. goverment   ☐   ________________________________

33. pronounciation   ☐   ________________________________

34. tempreture   ☐   ________________________________

35. according   ☐   ________________________________

36. vegtable   ☐   ________________________________

37. individual   ☐   ________________________________

38. restraunt   ☐   ________________________________

39. excellent   ☐   ________________________________

Complete the following tables, showing whether each word has been spelt correctly or incorrectly.

Examples:

WORD	Correct	Incorrect
lazy	☑	☐
funnie	☐	☑

WORD	Correct	Incorrect	WORD	Correct	Incorrect
40. dissapear	☐	☐	61. quarter	☐	☐
41. strenght	☐	☐	62. actually	☐	☐
42. build	☐	☐	63. thorugh	☐	☐
43. medcine	☐	☐	64. strange	☐	☐
44. excercise	☐	☐	65. suprise	☐	☐
45. group	☐	☐	66. popular	☐	☐
46. circle	☐	☐	67. rememember	☐	☐
47. straight	☐	☐	68. breathe	☐	☐
48. adress	☐	☐	69. consider	☐	☐
49. calander	☐	☐	70. deciede	☐	☐
50. seperate	☐	☐	71. certain	☐	☐
51. ordinray	☐	☐	72. pehaps	☐	☐
52. fruit	☐	☐	73. purpose	☐	☐
53. imagine	☐	☐	74. centry	☐	☐
54. paticular	☐	☐	75. intrest	☐	☐
55. hieght	☐	☐	76. important	☐	☐
56. learn	☐	☐	77. therefor	☐	☐
57. recent	☐	☐	78. sentance	☐	☐
58. natural	☐	☐	79. grammer	☐	☐
59. favorite	☐	☐	80. desperate	☐	☐
60. often	☐	☐	81. earth	☐	☐

> **Each of the following sentences contains ONE spelling mistake. Find the misspelt word and underline it.**
>
> ***Example:***   ***The young boy's behavior was terrible.***
>   *The young boy's <u>behavior</u> was terrible.*

82. Much controvesy surrounds this painting; many people believe it is a forgery.

83. We were all impressed by Maria's determinacion to compete in the race.

84. The meeting was interupted by the unexpected arrival of the police.

85. "Although it is ultimately your choice, I would not reccomend the fish," advised Tim.

86. One saying that my mother frequently uses is 'Curiousity killed the cat!'.

87. Every week, the villagers offered up a sacrafice to appease the ogre who lived nearby.

88. We must do everything we can to eradicate all forms of prejuidice all over the world.

89. The weather in Febuary and March is usually appalling.

90. Billy desprately wanted to be asked to join his school's athletics team.

91. Several members of the comittee walked out of the meeting in disgust.

92. This sauce makes a delicious accompniament to these grilled scallops.

93. Toni and Raja had a fierce arguement over who should have more responsibility.

94. Henry the Eight and his daughter, Elizabeth the First, are extremely famous English monarchs.

95. Keyla is bilingual as she speaks two langages fluently: Portuguese and English.

96. "Such occurences are very rare in the animal kingdom," said the zoologist.

97. I think there has been a failure of comunication between voters and politicians.

98. Recycling is a crucial means by which we can help preserve the enviroment.

99. This figurine is just a replica; the actuall sculpture is over 6 metres tall.

100. In all sinscerity, I don't believe that Anna and Rita are the culprits this time.

In each of the following, identify the words that are CORRECTLY spelt. Please note that, in some cases, you may need to select more than one option.

Examples:
- ____ _plate_
- ____ _spoon_
- ____ _fork_
- ____ _All 3 are incorrect_
- ✓ _All 3 are correct_

- ✓ _handbag_
- ____ _handel_
- ✓ _handwritten_
- ____ _All 3 are incorrect_
- ____ _All 3 are correct_

101.
- ____ ancient
- ____ system
- ____ diligent
- ____ All 3 are incorrect
- ____ All 3 are correct

102.
- ____ agressive
- ____ shoulder
- ____ center
- ____ All 3 are incorrect
- ____ All 3 are correct

103.
- ____ knowledge
- ____ conveneience
- ____ ryhthym
- ____ All 3 are incorrect
- ____ All 3 are correct

104.
- ____ averrage
- ____ complete
- ____ acsidentally
- ____ All 3 are incorrect
- ____ All 3 are correct

105.
- ____ especialy
- ____ perculiar
- ____ continue
- ____ All 3 are incorrect
- ____ All 3 are correct

106.
- ____ existance
- ____ oppotunity
- ____ dettatched
- ____ All 3 are incorrect
- ____ All 3 are correct

107.
- ____ describe
- ____ equippment
- ____ frequently
- ____ All 3 are incorrect
- ____ All 3 are correct

108.
- ____ sincerley
- ____ posession
- ____ minuite
- ____ All 3 are incorrect
- ____ All 3 are correct

109.
- ____ experiement
- ____ expereince
- ____ expertise
- ____ All 3 are incorrect
- ____ All 3 are correct

110.
- ____ develop
- ____ soldier
- ____ posibble
- ____ All 3 are incorrect
- ____ All 3 are correct

111.
- ____ parallel
- ____ histry
- ____ garde
- ____ All 3 are incorrect
- ____ All 3 are correct

112.
- ____ noughty
- ____ material
- ____ fowards
- ____ All 3 are incorrect
- ____ All 3 are correct

113.
- ____ mention
- ____ bicycle
- ____ appear
- ____ All 3 are incorrect
- ____ All 3 are correct

114.
- ____ libray
- ____ extream
- ____ supose
- ____ All 3 are incorrect
- ____ All 3 are correct

115.
- ____ rhyme
- ____ lenght
- ____ thought
- ____ All 3 are incorrect
- ____ All 3 are correct

In each of the following, choose the pair of correctly spelt words that completes the given sentence. Indicate your choice by writing the appropriate letter (A, B, C, or D) in the box provided.

Example: *Bettina* _______ *a magic cloak which made her* _______.

    A. possessed ... invissible   C. possest ... invisable
    B. posessed ... invisible   D. possessed ... invisible   **D**

116. The _______ was out of _______ because she had been running so hard.
    A. women ... breathe   C. woman ... breathe
    B. woman ... breath   D. womman ... breath

117. The _______ in our maths exam yesterday were more _______ than we expected.
    A. qestions ... difificult   C. questions ... difficult
    B. questcions ... dificult   D. questions ... difficulty

118. As the numbers of travellers _______, airports will become more _______.
    A. increases ... busy   C. increase ... buzy
    B. increses ... buisy   D. increase ... busy

119. If we _______ _______, we can get seats with a great view.
    A. arrive ... early   C. arive ... earely
    B. arrive ... earley   D. arrived ... earlie

120. Our _______ has _______ us a wonderful tour of Venice.
    A. guide ... promissed   C. guide ... promised
    B. giude ... prommised   D. guiude ... prommissed

121. Make sure you put _______ _______ on the wound to stop it bleeding.
    A. enought ... presurre   C. enaugh ... pressure
    B. enough ... pressure   D. enough ... pressur

122. The manager's _______ was pinned on the wall _______ the bathroom.
    A. nottice ... oppossite   C. notice ... opposit
    B. notise ... oppasite   D. notice ... opposite

123. The giant's _______ breathing was _______ interrupted by a few snores.
    A. regular ... occasionally   C. regular ... occassionally
    B. reguler ... ocassionally   D. regula ... occasionaly

124. The soldiers remained in their _______ even _______ they were terrified.
    A. possitions ... thought   C. positions ... though
    B. positions ... thouhg   D. posicions ... through

Some of the following words are missing a hyphen. Write out each word in the space provided, inserting a hyphen where necessary.

Examples: *deselect*   *deselect*

                     coown   *co-own*

1. reincarnation   _______________________

2. coincide   _______________________

3. antiinflammatory   _______________________

4. cooperation   _______________________

5. reimburse   _______________________

6. collaborate   _______________________

7. deemphasise   _______________________

8. deduce   _______________________

9. antihero   _______________________

10. reemploy   _______________________

11. recurring   _______________________

12. semicircle   _______________________

13. reduce   _______________________

14. collision   _______________________

15. redeem   _______________________

> In each of the following, use an appropriate prefix from the Prefix Bank with the root word supplied in brackets to create a correctly spelt new word that sensibly completes each sentence. Be careful: some cases require a hyphen, while others do not.
>
> **_Example:_** _As Jamila has changed her mind, we will have to _________ everything. (organise)_
> _As Jamila has changed her mind, we will have to <u>reorganise</u> everything._

PREFIX BANK

co-　　　de-　　　re-　　　semi-　　　anti-　　　micro-

16. Spacecraft become extremely hot when they ______________ our atmosphere. (enter)

17. I have terrible hand-eye ____________________. (ordination)

18. The thieves used __________________ weapons during the bank robbery. (automatic)

19. The engineers at Apple have __________________ the iPhone's software. (designed)

20. Indira wants to become a ____________________ when she is older. (biologist)

21. Hopefully, this summit will help __________________ the crisis. (escalate)

22. Your essay needs __________________; it's still full of mistakes. (editing)

23. One way your body keeps you healthy is by producing __________________. (bodies)

24. Gill and Richard are the ____________________ of the town gala. (organisers)

25. The __________________ is a difficult punctuation mark to use. (colon)

26. The lieutenant was __________________ because of his irresponsibility. (moted)

27. After 10 years, the police are __________________ the unsolved case. (examining)

28. "Don't be __________________, Pippa. Come and join us," her mother said. (social)

29. Mr Smith is hoping to be __________________ as the leader of his party. (elected)

30. The elves had to __________________ with the fairies to beat the goblins. (operate)

31. Bacteria are a type of ____________________. (organism)

In each of the following words, either the letters _ie_ or _ei_ have been removed. Decide which pair correctly completes each word, and then write the correctly spelt word in the space provided.

**Example:**   pr___st   _priest_

1. fr____nd   ________________________

2. l____sure   ________________________

3. anx____ty   ________________________

4. conven____nt   ________________________

5. r____gn   ________________________

6. fr____ght   ________________________

7. for____gn   ________________________

8. ____derdown   ________________________

9. impat____nt   ________________________

10. br____fcase   ________________________

11. w____ght   ________________________

12. n____ghbourhood   ________________________

13. y____ld   ________________________

14. r____ndeer   ________________________

15. sover____gn   ________________________

16. hyg____ne   ________________________

17. gondol____r   ________________________

> **Show whether each sentence contains a spelling mistake or not. Use a tick to show the sentence is correct (☑) or a cross to show that it is not (☒).**
>
> **_Examples:_** **_The feild was full of sunflowers._**   ☒
>   **_There was a brief shocked silence before everyone started to argue._**   ☑

18. You should always be quiet when you are in a library.   ☐

19. We were all relieved to discover that we had passed our exams.   ☐

20. Ibrahim saw an opportunity and siezed it with both hands.   ☐

21. The Roman army beseiged the town for months.   ☐

22. The banks have warned us to be on the look-out for counterfeit money.   ☐

23. Kim's birthday is on the eighteenth of September.   ☐

24. Surprisingly few people came to the unvieling of the town's new monument.   ☐

25. Seaweed is an ingredeint that is commonly used in the Far East.   ☐

26. Dorothy grabbed the reins of her horse and vaulted into the saddle.   ☐

27. The headmaster was surprisingly leneint with the troublemakers.   ☐

28. All of the king's subjects grieved when he died.   ☐

29. I don't know the difference between a brigadier and a leiutenant.   ☐

30. Pieces of glass fell off the chandeleir during the earthquake.   ☐

31. Some people believe that other planets are inhabited by aliens.   ☐

32. Fran's neice is a very disobedient child.   ☐

33. The poltergeist made some extremely weird noises.   ☐

34. The findings of the newest scientific report have not been well-recieved.   ☐

35. Mrs Green likes drinking decaffeinated coffee in a biege mug.   ☐

> **In each of the following, choose the pair of correctly spelt words that completes the given sentence. Indicate your choice by writing the appropriate letter (A, B, C, or D) in the box provided.**
>
> _Example:_ Jo's _______ is most _______ .
>
> A. behaviour … vexacious   C. behaviour … vexatious
> B. behaiviour … vexatious   D. behavior … vexacious
>
> [C]

1. The _______ elf _______ forward carefully.
   A. cautious … tiptoed   C. causious … tiptoeded
   B. caucious … tiptode   D. cuatious … tiptoad

2. The _______ wolves encircled the _______ deer.
   A. vitious … defensless   C. vicious … defenseless
   B. vitious … deffenceless   D. vicious … defenceless

3. The honest _______ delivered the _______ cargo to the merchant.
   A. sailer … pretious   C. saylor … preshous
   B. sailor … precious   D. sailor … prescious

4. _______ food doesn't have to be _______ .
   A. Nutricious … inappetising   C. Newtritious … unapettising
   B. Nutriscious … inapettising   D. Nutritious … unappetising

5. The film we saw at the cinema was extremely _______ as it was very _______ .
   A. boring … repetitious   C. borring … repititious
   B. boreing … repeticious   D. boring … reppitious

6. The story William told us was _______; it was utterly _______ .
   A. nonesense … ficticious   C. nonsense … fictitious
   B. nonesense … fictitious   D. nonsense … fictious

7. The _______ scope of this novel makes it no less _______ .
   A. ambicious … menotonous   C. ambitious … monotinous
   B. ambitious … monotonous   D. ambicious … monotenous

8. The ballroom was both _______ and _______ .
   A. spatious … luxsurious   C. spacious … luxurious
   B. spacious … luxiurious   D. spatious … luxorious

9. Although Ingrid is a _______ reader, she is an _______ speller.
   A. veracious … atrocious   C. voratious … atrotious
   B. voracious … atrotious   D. voracious … atrocious

> **In each of the following, identify the words that are CORRECTLY spelt. Please note that, in some cases, you may need to select more than one option.**
>
> _**Examples:**_   ____ *plate*   ✓ *handbag*
>   ____ *spoon*   ____ *handel*
>   ____ *fork*   ✓ *handwritten*
>   ____ *All 3 are incorrect*   ____ *All 3 are incorrect*
>   ✓ *All 3 are correct*   ____ *All 3 are correct*

10.	11.	12.
___ delitious	___ famous	___ anxious
___ malitious	___ various	___ suspicious
___ curious	___ poisonous	___ adventrous
___ All 3 are incorrect	___ All 3 are incorrect	___ All 3 are incorrect
___ All 3 are correct	___ All 3 are correct	___ All 3 are correct

13.	14.	15.
___ superstitious	___ mountanous	___ humungous
___ barbarious	___ dangerous	___ conscious
___ hideous	___ perilous	___ hazzardous
___ All 3 are incorrect	___ All 3 are incorrect	___ All 3 are incorrect
___ All 3 are correct	___ All 3 are correct	___ All 3 are correct

16.	17.	18.
___ in-famous	___ tremendous	___ precarious
___ lushous	___ outragious	___ precipitous
___ marvelous	___ jealous	___ precocious
___ All 3 are incorrect	___ All 3 are incorrect	___ All 3 are incorrect
___ All 3 are correct	___ All 3 are correct	___ All 3 are correct

19.	20.	21.
___ tedious	___ gracious	___ vigourous
___ joyous	___ infectious	___ trecherous
___ glamarous	___ anonymous	___ venomous
___ All 3 are incorrect	___ All 3 are incorrect	___ All 3 are incorrect
___ All 3 are correct	___ All 3 are correct	___ All 3 are correct

22.	23.	24.
___ ridiculous	___ fabbulous	___ prosprous
___ thundrous	___ disasterous	___ rebbelious
___ herbiverous	___ pretencious	___ stuppendous
___ All 3 are incorrect	___ All 3 are incorrect	___ All 3 are incorrect
___ All 3 are correct	___ All 3 are correct	___ All 3 are correct

For each of the following, select the one correct spelling from the choices given.

Example: *The only piece of evidence the police had was _______.*

    A. *circumstancial*   B. *circamstantial*   (C.) *circumstantial*   D. *circumstantiall*

1.   Learning to spell well is an ___________ skill.
    A. essential   B. essencial   C. essenntial   D. essenncial

2.   You can't read that letter; it's ___________ !
    A. confedential   B. confidencial   C. confidential   D. confiddential

3.   Lots of ___________ ingredients are bad for us.
    A. artifitial   B. arteficial   C. artifiscial   D. artificial

4.   Many important ___________ attended the meeting with the Prime Minister.
    A. officials   B. offitials   C. oficcials   D. ofiscials

5.   The shepherd had a very ___________ accent.
    A. provintial   B. provincial   C. provinncial   D. provential

6.   The children had prepared a ___________ surprise for their mother's birthday.
    A. spescial   B. speciel   C. special   D. speicial

7.   We live in a quiet, ___________ area.
    A. resedential   B. residencial   C. residential   D. resedencial

8.   The unfeeling step-mother gave the child a ___________ stare.
    A. glacial   B. glasial   C. glatial   D. galacial

9.   Many young people nowadays get their news from ___________ media.
    A. soscial   B. soccial   C. sotial   D. social

10. Today, we watched several interesting ___________.
    A. infommercials   B. infomercials   C. infomertials   D. informmertials

All of the following words end with either the letters **-cial** or **-tial**. Use the clues given to help you work out what each word is. Then, fill in the missing letters of the word so that it is spelt correctly.

Example: **First**   i n _ _ _ _ l
        First   i n *i* *t* *i* *a* l

11. On the surface   s ___ p ___ ___ f ___ ___ ___ ___ ___

12. Relating to money   f ___ n ___ n ___ ___ ___ ___

13. A bit of something   p ___ r ___ ___ ___ ___

14. Relating to trade   c o m ___ ___ ___ ___ ___ ___ ___

15. Possible   p ___ t ___ ___ ___ ___ ___ ___

16. In order   s ___ q u ___ n ___ ___ ___ ___

17. Relating to race   r ___ ___ ___ ___ ___

18. Like a palace   p ___ l ___ ___ ___ ___ ___

19. Very important   c r ___ ___ ___ ___ ___

20. Having influence   i ___ f l ___ ___ ___ ___ ___ ___ ___

21. Particular   e s p ___ ___ ___ ___ ___

22. Relating to war   m a ___ ___ ___ ___ ___

23. Unbiased; fair   i m p ___ ___ ___ ___ ___ ___

24. Relating to the face f ___ ___ ___ ___ ___

25. Not authorized   u n o ___ ___ ___ ___ ___ ___ ___

26. Having good results b ___ n ___ f ___ ___ ___ ___ ___

27. Relating to a judge j ___ d ___ ___ ___ ___ ___

28. Of real value   s ___ b s ___ ___ ___ ___ ___ ___ ___

See how well you remember the spellings of the words in Units 1-5! In all of the following tests, show whether each word is correct or incorrect.

Examples: hello   ☑

               wellcome   ☒

TEST 6.1

1. accident ☐
2. awkword ☐
3. barbrous ☐
4. calendar ☐
5. compleat ☐
6. de-duce ☐
7. excellant ☐
8. greived ☐
9. jealous ☐
10. martial ☐
11. occassion ☐
12. parallel ☐
13. pressure ☐
14. quiet ☐
15. sacrafice ☐
16. suspitious ☐
17. twelth ☐
18. unofficial ☐
19. variaty ☐
20. weight ☐

SCORE _______ /20

TEST 6.2

1. acompany ☐
2. averrage ☐
3. beige ☐
4. category ☐
5. confidencial ☐
6. de-emphasise ☐
7. exerscise ☐
8. glamorous ☐
9. impartial ☐
10. mallicious ☐
11. occupy ☐
12. particuler ☐
13. potential ☐
14. relevent ☐
15. redeam ☐
16. sceintific ☐
17. supprise ☐
18. suppose ☐
19. tremmendous ☐
20. vigerous ☐

SCORE _______ /20

TEST 6.3

1. adventureous ☐
2. arrive ☐
3. beleive ☐
4. cautious ☐
5. curriosity ☐
6. desparate ☐
7. eighteenth ☐
8. Februray ☐
9. glacial ☐
10. impatiant ☐
11. length ☐
12. mention ☐
13. neice ☐
14. officials ☐
15. physical ☐
16. prescious ☐
17. residential ☐
18. redeseigned ☐
19. sincere ☐
20. wierd ☐

SCORE _______ /20

TEST 6.4

1. aliens ☐
2. anxiety ☐
3. benificial ☐
4. century ☐
5. controvasy ☐
6. dictionary ☐
7. especiall ☐
8. favourate ☐
9. gondolier ☐
10. harrassed ☐
11. increase ☐
12. leisure ☐
13. microbiolagist ☐
14. nutricious ☐
15. opposite ☐
16. pieces ☐
17. prosprous ☐
18. reduce ☐
19. re-elected ☐
20. semiautomatic ☐
21. superfficial ☐
22. vennomous ☐

SCORE _______ /22

TEST 6.5

1. ambicious ☐
2. arguement ☐
3. beseiged ☐
4. chandelier ☐
5. convienience ☐
6. dissappear ☐
7. existance ☐
8. facial ☐
9. hazadous ☐
10. infammous ☐
11. library ☐
12. marvellous ☐
13. ordinery ☐
14. poisonous ☐
15. purpose ☐
16. recent ☐
17. re-employ ☐
18. semicircle ☐
19. soveriegn ☐
20. tedious ☐
21. unveilling ☐
22. well-recieved ☐

SCORE _______ /22

TEST 6.6

1. antibodies ☐
2. atroscious ☐
3. bicycle ☐
4. co-incide ☐
5. co-operate ☐
6. died ☐
7. experiment ☐
8. finnancial ☐
9. herbiverous ☐
10. infectious ☐
11. lenient ☐
12. leiutenant ☐
13. minuite ☐
14. possesion ☐
15. quarter ☐
16. ryhthm ☐
17. reenter ☐
18. regular ☐
19. racial ☐
20. seized ☐
21. superstious ☐
22. vicious ☐

SCORE _______ /22

TEST 6.7

1. ammateur ☐
2. artiffical ☐
3. breathe ☐
4. collaborrate ☐
5. coordinaition ☐
6. deliscious ☐
7. extreame ☐
8. essential ☐
9. fictitous ☐
10. hiddeous ☐
11. influential ☐
12. knowledge ☐
13. luscious ☐
14. microorganism ☐
15. notice ☐
16. outragious ☐
17. partial ☐
18. possible ☐
19. reins ☐
20. remember ☐
21. speciall ☐
22. unappettising ☐

SCORE _______ /22

TEST 6.8

1. address ☐
2. appear ☐
3. briefcase ☐
4. collision ☐
5. counterfiet ☐
6. desperetely ☐
7. experience ☐
8. eigth ☐
9. forewards ☐
10. humungous ☐
11. info-mercials ☐
12. luxiurious ☐
13. mountanous ☐
14. perculiar ☐
15. prejudice ☐
16. queue ☐
17. relieved ☐
18. repeticious ☐
19. sinscerely ☐
20. signiture ☐
21. tomorow ☐
22. various ☐

SCORE _______ /22

TEST 6.9

1. antiheroe ☐
2. anxious ☐
3. briggadier ☐
4. commercial ☐
5. conssious ☐
6. disasterous ☐
7. equippment ☐
8. especialy ☐
9. foreign ☐
10. goverment ☐
11. hygeine ☐
12. ingredeient ☐
13. naughty ☐
14. opportunity ☐
15. perillous ☐
16. provincial ☐
17. ryhme ☐
18. restaraunt ☐
19. re-examinning ☐
20. secratary ☐
21. social ☐
22. thundrous ☐

SCORE _______ /22

TEST 6.10

1. acciddentally ☐
2. agressive ☐
3. brusied ☐
4. comittee ☐
5. co-organisers ☐
6. criticises ☐
7. determinacion ☐
8. enviroment ☐
9. explaination ☐
10. friend ☐
11. gracious ☐
12. neccessary ☐
13. palatial ☐
14. programe ☐
15. reccurring ☐
16. reigndeer ☐
17. ridiculous ☐
18. spatious ☐
19. substancial ☐
20. sentence ☐
21. therefor ☐
22. Wendnesday ☐

SCORE ______ /22

TEST 6.11

1. accompianment ☐
2. anonymous ☐
3. communication ☐
4. co-operation ☐
5. crucial ☐
6. demmoted ☐
7. disobiedient ☐
8. embarass ☐
9. frequently ☐
10. grammer ☐
11. monotonous ☐
12. occurences ☐
13. parlament ☐
14. pretensious ☐
15. recomend ☐
16. re-editing ☐
17. reign ☐
18. semicollon ☐
19. sequential ☐
20. sinscerity ☐
21. tempareture ☐
22. yeild ☐

SCORE ______ /22

TEST 6.12

1. anti-inflamatory ☐
2. antisocial ☐
3. competition ☐
4. conveinient ☐
5. curious ☐
6. decafeinated ☐
7. de-escalated ☐
8. eiderdown ☐
9. expertise ☐
10. freight ☐
11. guarrantee ☐
12. judicial ☐
13. neighborhood ☐
14. ocassionally ☐
15. poltergiest ☐
16. pronounciation ☐
17. reincarnation ☐
18. rebelious ☐
19. reimburse ☐
20. stupendous ☐
21. trecherous ☐
22. voracious ☐

SCORE ______ /22

Complete the following statements using the prefix <u>dis-</u>, <u>mis-</u>, <u>il-</u>, or <u>ir-</u>. Then write the correctly spelt word in the space provided.

Example: ___ + *take* ⇨ __________

       <u>mis</u> + *take* ⇨ <u>mistake</u>

1. _____ + courage ⇨ ________________
2. _____ + lead ⇨ ________________
3. _____ + relevant ⇨ ________________
4. _____ + behave ⇨ ________________
5. _____ + possess ⇨ ________________
6. _____ + print ⇨ ________________
7. _____ + address ⇨ ________________
8. _____ + regular ⇨ ________________
9. _____ + obey ⇨ ________________
10. _____ + govern ⇨ ________________
11. _____ + legal ⇨ ________________
12. _____ + count ⇨ ________________
13. _____ + agree ⇨ ________________
14. _____ + guide ⇨ ________________
15. _____ + heard ⇨ ________________
16. _____ + appoint ⇨ ________________

17. _____ + legible ⇨ ________________
18. _____ + rational ⇨ ________________
19. _____ + allow ⇨ ________________
20. _____ + regard ⇨ ________________
21. _____ + pose ⇨ ________________
22. _____ + fit ⇨ ________________
23. _____ + shaped ⇨ ________________
24. _____ + arm ⇨ ________________
25. _____ + able ⇨ ________________
26. _____ + align ⇨ ________________
27. _____ + conduct ⇨ ________________
28. _____ + card ⇨ ________________
29. _____ + grace ⇨ ________________
30. _____ + honest ⇨ ________________
31. _____ + handle ⇨ ________________
32. _____ + label ⇨ ________________

NONE of the following words have been spelt correctly. Write the correct spelling of each word in the space provided.

33. ilitterate _______________

34. disaproval _______________

35. mispelled _______________

36. iresponsible _______________

37. dissapearence _______________

38. misremmember _______________

39. disatisfied _______________

40. discontinueing _______________

41. mistreatmant _______________

42. disadvantege _______________

43. disaggreeible _______________

44. ilogicall _______________

45. mistrustfull _______________

46. irrisitible _______________

47. dissapointmant _______________

48. misaprehention _______________

49. misdead _______________

50. irreversable _______________

51. mislayd _______________

52. disembarcked _______________

53. discourtious _______________

54. misdirrection _______________

55. disasembile _______________

56. discomfurt _______________

57. misinfomation _______________

58. disinchanted _______________

59. misconseption _______________

60. disimilarity _______________

61. misaplied _______________

62. disrupcion _______________

63. mispeak _______________

64. disordaly _______________

65. misjudgded _______________

66. dismissel _______________

67. illegitemate _______________

68. disbeleivingly _______________

In each of the following, show whether the given word is spelt correctly or incorrectly. If the word is incorrectly spelt, write the correct spelling in the space provided.

**Examples:**   *ancient*   ☑   ________

                   neice   ☒   *niece*

1. concieve   ☐   _______________________________

2. mischeivous   ☐   _______________________________

3. conscience   ☐   _______________________________

4. species   ☐   _______________________________

5. cieling   ☐   _______________________________

6. achievement   ☐   _______________________________

7. nuclei   ☐   _______________________________

8. societies   ☐   _______________________________

9. juciest   ☐   _______________________________

10. conceirge   ☐   _______________________________

11. piecemeal   ☐   _______________________________

12. reicipts   ☐   _______________________________

13. glacier   ☐   _______________________________

14. financeir   ☐   _______________________________

15. peircingly   ☐   _______________________________

16. deceivers   ☐   _______________________________

17. recipies   ☐   _______________________________

18. deficiency   ☐   _______________________________

19. omniscient   ☐   _______________________________

20. transcievers   ☐   _______________________________

21. concietedness   ☐   _______________________________

22. unperceived   ☐   _______________________________

Many of the following words have Greek or Latin origins. Carefully read the words in each group, then answer the question beneath them. Write your answer in the space provided.

Example: *science   discipline   inescapable   ascend*
   In which word are the letters 'sc' pronounced differently?   *inescapable*

1. scheme chorus charity anarchy
    In which word are the letters 'ch' pronounced differently?   ______________________

2. crypt calypso lyric psyche
    In which word is the letter 'y' pronounced differently?   ______________________

3. mascot crescent cascade fiasco
    In which word are the letters 'sc' pronounced differently?   ______________________

4. cyanide photosynthesis syndicate synonym
    In which word is the letter 'y' pronounced differently?   ______________________

5. Achilles bronchitis enchilada monarchy
    In which word are the letters 'ch' pronounced differently?   ______________________

6. symbol rye typical symptom
    In which word is the letter 'y' pronounced differently?   ______________________

7. martyr sty pyre typhoon
    In which word is the letter 'y' pronounced differently?   ______________________

8. obscene adolescent scimitar crescendo
    In which word are the letters 'sc' pronounced differently?   ______________________

9. chided urchins archipelago besmirched
    In which word are the letters 'ch' pronounced differently?   ______________________

10. gymkhana gyroscope hymn gymnasium
    In which word is the letter 'y' pronounced differently?   ______________________

11. hibiscus escapade fresco fluorescent
    In which word are the letters 'sc' pronounced differently?   ______________________

> Each underlined word below has either a Greek or Latin origin. Show whether each underlined word is spelt correctly or not. Use a tick to show the word is correct (☑) or a cross to show that it is not (☒).
>
> _**Examples:**_   _The ship's <u>anchor</u> was covered with barnacles._   ☑
>   _Google <u>Crome</u> is the name of a very popular web browser._   ☒

12. Although the portrait was <u>asymetrical</u>, it was still beautiful to look at. ☐

13. The politician was extremely popular because she was so <u>charismatic</u>. ☐

14. The rebels' <u>scheames</u> were discovered by the king's spies. ☐

15. Two sides of an <u>isosseles</u> triangle are equal in length. ☐

16. Car drivers should always be aware that there may be <u>cyclists</u> on the road. ☐

17. Penny went to a concert with her mother to hear a famous <u>orchestra</u> play. ☐

18. The strange noise kept <u>ecchoing</u> around the vast cave. ☐

19. <u>Crysanthemums</u> are among my favourite flowers. ☐

20. Our class went to see a play with wonderful <u>scenary</u> at the Old Vic. ☐

21. The duck-billed <u>platipus</u> is an interesting, but peculiar, semi-aquatic creature. ☐

22. Although many children love <u>effervescent</u> drinks, they are usually full of sugar. ☐

23. The famous Pyramid of Djoser was designed by Imhotep, the <u>arcitecht</u>. ☐

24. I have always been <u>suseptible</u> to headaches. ☐

25. Holding his <u>scepter</u> aloft, the emperor declared the start of the Games. ☐

26. The eyes of the <u>chameleon</u> can move in different directions at the same time. ☐

27. Gerhardt decided that he wanted to learn how to play the <u>tympani</u>. ☐

28. A suspicious-looking <u>character</u> was loitering in the park, so Ida called the police. ☐

29. Desiderius Erasmus was a famous Dutch <u>scolar</u> who was born in 1466. ☐

30. Historians used to believe that medieval society was exceedingly <u>heirarchical</u>. ☐

One word in each of the following sentences is a word of French origin that is missing a letter string. Read the sentence carefully to work out what the word is. Then, fill in the missing letters so that the word is spelt correctly.

Example: *Amanda made us a delicious q______e for supper.*
              Amanda made us a delicious quiche for supper.

31. The restaurant's fabulous new c______________f is Italian.

32. The rude boy stuck out his t______________e at the kindly old man.

33. The pantomime villain had a huge beard and a twirly m______________e.

34. This sculpture is u______________e; there isn't another one like it in the world.

35. Our washing m______________e has broken down again.

36. Hal has become a member of the Essex Junior Football L______________e.

37. Jamie received a holiday b______________e from Thomas Cook.

38. The skydiver opened her p______________e after she jumped out of the aeroplane.

39. Last summer, Ivan spent a month in a c______________t in Switzerland.

40. Jamila has an a______________e bowl that is over two hundred years old.

41. The manager thanked all of his c__________s for their hard work.

42. Kelly's b______________e sells a collection of vintage and second-hand clothes.

43. The Black Death is the name of a deadly fourteenth-century p______________e.

44. King Arthur's knights were famous for their c______________y.

45. Mark bought Tiffany a beautiful b______________t of flowers for her birthday.

46. Hanging from the ceiling was a wonderful crystal c______________r.

47. We will send you our monthly c______________e full of our latest products.

48. Liam is allergic to p______________o nuts.

49. Ahmed went to the bank to cash the c______________e his uncle had given him.

> Many of the following words have French origins. Carefully read the words in each group, then answer the question beneath them. Write your answer in the space provided.
>
> _**Example:**_ _delinquent   conquer   squelch   queen_
> _**In which word are the letters 'que' pronounced differently?**_   _conquer_

50. picturesque consequence quest squeak
    In which word are the letters 'que' pronounced differently?   _______________

51. bewitch challenge archer champagne
    In which word are the letters 'ch' pronounced differently?   _______________

52. banquet racquet prequel squelch
    In which word are the letters 'que' pronounced differently?   _______________

53. query aqueduct physique queasy
    In which word are the letters 'que' pronounced differently?   _______________

54. orchid chlorine stomach fuchsia
    In which word are the letters 'ch' pronounced differently?   _______________

55. request grotesque squeeze frequent
    In which word are the letters 'que' pronounced differently?   _______________

56. arachnid chaperone machete chivalrous
    In which word are the letters 'ch' pronounced differently?   _______________

57. technique mosque question plaque
    In which word are the letters 'que' pronounced differently?   _______________

58. avalanche crochet crèche archive
    In which word are the letters 'ch' pronounced differently?   _______________

59. chic chasm chauffeur charade
    In which word are the letters 'ch' pronounced differently?   _______________

60. bequeath equestrian querulous opaque
    In which word are the letters 'que' pronounced differently?   _______________

> **In each of the following, add the word ending _-ly_ or _-ally_ to each root word given in brackets. Make any necessary changes, then use the correctly spelt word to complete the sentence.**
>
> _**Example:**_ _"I think I have done very ________ in my exam," moaned Rita. (bad)_
>   _"I think I have done very <u>badly</u> in my exam," moaned Rita. (bad)_

1. The politicians were all ________________________________ elected. (democratic)

2. The twins, Jo and Kit, went to the party ________________________________. (separate)

3. You shouldn't judge other people too ________________________________. (harsh)

4. The old man shook his head ____________________________ at the foolish knight. (grave)

5. ____________________________, Samantha agreed to help clean the kitchen. (begrudging)

6. "Don't take Bob too ____________________________," Dot advised Nina. (literal)

7. As the phone was made so ____________________________, it broke very quickly. (flimsy)

8. The Fairy Queen ____________________________ made us disappear. (magic)

9. He believed ____________________________ that everything was going to be fine. (naive)

10. Tim argued ____________________________ that he should be given a new X-Box. (persuasive)

11. "Such behaviour is ____________________________ unacceptable!" said Gina. (complete)

12. The fans behaved ____________________________ when their team lost. (abominable)

13. The clients ____________________________ agreed to the terms of the contract. (ready)

14. ____________________________ speaking, that is not true at all. (historic)

15. ____________________________, I go to bed at 11 pm. (ordinary)

16. "I will meet you at six o'clock ____________________________," he promised. (precise)

17. "The worm will return," Sherlock Holmes said ____________________________. (cryptic)

18. "Help...me," whispered the wounded soldier ____________________________. (hoarse)

19. All our products are ____________________________ friendly. (environment)

> **In each of the following, you are given the definition of a word. Select the one correct spelling of the word that is being defined from the choices given.**
>
> _Example:_ _In a fitting, or an appropriate, manner_
>
> A. *suitabley*   B. *suitibly*   C. *suitabally*   (D.) *suitably*

20. In a very sad, depressed, or despondent way
     A. misrabaly   B. misarebly   C. misrebly   D. miserably

21. In an uncomplicated or simple way
     A. basicly   B. basically   C. basiscaly   D. basecly

22. In an instantaneous manner
     A. immediatley   B. immediatly   C. immediately   D. immedietley

23. In a happy way
     A. cheerily   B. cheeryly   C. cheerilly   D. cheerally

24. In a manner that cannot be explained
     A. inexplicabally   B. inexplicibly   C. inexplicably   D. inexplicabably

25. In a solemn and self-important manner
     A. pomposly   B. pompusally   C. pompusly   D. pompously

26. In a scholarly way or fashion
     A. academicly   B. academically   C. accademically   D. accademicly

27. In a way that only lasts for a limited period of time
     A. temporarally   B. temperarily   C. temperarally   D. temporarily

28. In a material, definite, or real way
     A. tangibly   B. tangeably   C. tangibally   D. tangebally

29. In a complex or complicated way
     A. elabourately   B. elaboratly   C. elaborately   D. elaborateley

Complete the following statements using either the suffix **-able** or **-ible**. Then write the correctly spelt word — having made any necessary changes — in the space provided.

Examples: *reason +* ___ ⇨ __________   *reduce +* ___ ⇨ __________

        reason + _able_ ⇨ _reasonable_   *reduce +* _ible_ ⇨ _reducible_

1. prevent + _____ ⇨ ______________
2. envy + _____ ⇨ ______________
3. apply + _____ ⇨ ______________
4. mention + _____ ⇨ ______________
5. adore + _____ ⇨ ______________
6. question + _____ ⇨ ______________
7. admit + _____ ⇨ ______________
8. reverse + _____ ⇨ ______________
9. like + _____ ⇨ ______________
10. answer + _____ ⇨ ______________
11. construct + _____ ⇨ ______________
12. imagine + _____ ⇨ ______________
13. deny + _____ ⇨ ______________
14. attach + _____ ⇨ ______________
15. deduce + _____ ⇨ ______________
16. regret + _____ ⇨ ______________

17. knowledge + _____ ⇨ ______________
18. recommend + _____ ⇨ ______________
19. programme + _____ ⇨ ______________
20. achieve + _____ ⇨ ______________
21. vary + _____ ⇨ ______________
22. access + _____ ⇨ ______________
23. breathe + _____ ⇨ ______________
24. suggest + _____ ⇨ ______________
25. collapse + _____ ⇨ ______________
26. destruct + _____ ⇨ ______________
27. tolerate + _____ ⇨ ______________
28. suppose + _____ ⇨ ______________
29. divide + _____ ⇨ ______________
30. consume + _____ ⇨ ______________
31. collect + _____ ⇨ ______________
32. appreciate + _____ ⇨ ______________

In each of the following, choose the pair of correctly spelt words that completes the given sentence. Indicate your choice by writing the appropriate letter (A, B, C, or D) in the box provided.

Example: That ______ is ______.

    A. materiall ... flamable   C. matterial ... flamible
    B. material ... flammable   D. meterial ... flamable

    B

33. The ______ Hilda reached was highly ______.
    A. conclusion ... debatible   C. conclusion ... debatable
    B. conclucion ... debatably   D. conclution ... dibatable

34. The ______ caused by the tropical storm was ______ greater than we thought.
    A. dammage ... consideribly   C. dammige ... considerabley
    B. damage ... considerably   D. damadge ... considrably

35. For once, the ______ put forward by Mandy was ______ made.
    A. suggestian ... sensibley   C. suggestion ... senseabley
    B. sugestion ... sensably   D. suggestion ... sensibly

36. That chair is not particularly ______; I think we should ______ a new one.
    A. comfortable ... purchase   C. comfortible ... purchous
    B. comftable ... perchase   D. comftible ... purchase

37. The handwriting in the book was barely ______; it was almost ______ to read.
    A. leggible ... impossable   C. legable ... imposssible
    B. legiable ... impossible   D. legible ... impossible

38. The weather has not been ______ recently; it's been extremely ______.
    A. reliable ... changable   C. relyible ... changible
    B. reliable ... changeable   D. relyable ... changeable

39. Brutus' speech was a ______ reminder of how ______ people could be.
    A. forceable ... pesuadable   C. forcible ... persuadable
    B. forceible ... persuadible   D. forcibel ... persuadeible

40. My favourite TV series is ______ ______; every episode is always entertaining.
    A. dependibly ... enjoyible   C. dependably ... enjoyable
    B. dependabley ... injoyable   D. dipendably ... enjoiable

41. Martin's behaviour has changed ______, which is completely ______.
    A. noticeably ... understandable   C. noticeably ... understandible
    B. notibly ... understandable   D. noticably ... understandable

See how well you remember the correct spellings of the words in Units 7-11! In all of the following tests, show whether each word is correct or incorrect.

Examples: *hello*   ☑

                 wellcome   ☒

TEST 12.1

1. acheivable ☐
2. architect ☐
3. basically ☐
4. cheerily ☐
5. crypt ☐
6. colleaugues ☐
7. dissable ☐
8. discount ☐
9. elabourately ☐
10. grave ☐
11. hoarse ☐
12. imediately ☐
13. juicest ☐
14. literral ☐
15. magic ☐
16. misaddress ☐
17. misconduct ☐
18. precise ☐
19. physique ☐
20. ready ☐

SCORE _______ /20

TEST 12.2

1. accessable ☐
2. archive ☐
3. bancquet ☐
4. complete ☐
5. consequence ☐
6. champaigne ☐
7. disaggree ☐
8. discouradge ☐
9. frequent ☐
10. glacier ☐
11. harsh ☐
12. imaginable ☐
13. ill-logical ☐
14. misalign ☐
15. mischievious ☐
16. misdirection ☐
17. naive ☐
18. pesuasive ☐
19. raquet ☐
20. scepter ☐

SCORE _______ /20

TEST 12.3

1. abhominable ☐
2. begrudgeing ☐
3. concieve ☐
4. collectibal ☐
5. chandalier ☐
6. chasm ☐
7. disallow ☐
8. dissappoint ☐
9. disgrace ☐
10. finnancier ☐
11. historic ☐
12. ir-rational ☐
13. leaugue ☐
14. missfit ☐
15. mispelt ☐
16. miseribly ☐
17. ordinary ☐
18. pierceingly ☐
19. parashute ☐
20. request ☐

SCORE _______ /20

TEST 12.4

1. academically ☐
2. avalanch ☐
3. boutique ☐
4. constructible ☐
5. chorous ☐
6. charactar ☐
7. decievers ☐
8. dissapearance ☐
9. dishonest ☐
10. enjoyible ☐
11. fiasco ☐
12. irregular ☐
13. legible ☐
14. missapplied ☐
15. mentionible ☐
16. mishandle ☐
17. plauge ☐
18. receipts ☐
19. scheame ☐
20. squeltch ☐
21. tollerable ☐
22. typical ☐

SCORE _______ /22

TEST 12.5

1. admissable ☐
2. attachable ☐
3. consummable ☐
4. cascade ☐
5. chameleon ☐
6. deduceable ☐
7. dissaproval ☐
8. disobey ☐
9. flimsy ☐
10. gymmasium ☐
11. inexpliccably ☐
12. misbehave ☐
13. misinfomation ☐
14. mislayed ☐
15. mispeak ☐
16. persuasively ☐
17. quest ☐
18. regretable ☐
19. societys ☐
20. symbol ☐
21. scholar ☐
22. scenary ☐

SCORE _______ /22

TEST 12.6

1. adoreable ☐
2. aprecciate ☐
3. cryptical ☐
4. comfortible ☐
5. ceiling ☐
6. demacratic ☐
7. dissasemble ☐
8. dispose ☐
9. environment ☐
10. hymn ☐
11. impossible ☐
12. iliterate ☐
13. likeable ☐
14. misconception ☐
15. misjudged ☐
16. piecemeal ☐
17. picturesque ☐
18. readilly ☐
19. sepparate ☐
20. suggestion ☐
21. synonnym ☐
22. transcievers ☐

SCORE _______ /22

TEST 12.7

1. answerable ☐
2. acqueduct ☐
3. collapsable ☐
4. concsience ☐
5. chaperrone ☐
6. denible ☐
7. dissmisal ☐
8. disorderly ☐
9. forcible ☐
10. gravely ☐
11. iresponsible ☐
12. magically ☐
13. misgovern ☐
14. moustasche ☐
15. mishaped ☐
16. platypus ☐
17. persuadible ☐
18. query ☐
19. reliable ☐
20. suppossable ☐
21. symptom ☐
22. tangeably ☐

SCORE _______ /22

TEST 12.8

1. appliccable ☐
2. anarchy ☐
3. conceierge ☐
4. changeable ☐
5. carismatic ☐
6. destructable ☐
7. disregard ☐
8. enviable ☐
9. harshly ☐
10. irrellevant ☐
11. knowledgable ☐
12. misheard ☐
13. nuclei ☐
14. ordinarily ☐
15. preventible ☐
16. pompously ☐
17. recommendible ☐
18. species ☐
19. technicque ☐
20. typhoon ☐
21. temporrarily ☐
22. understandable ☐

SCORE _______ /22

TEST 12.9

1. apprecible ☐
2. asymmetrical ☐
3. brochure ☐
4. conclusion ☐
5. checque ☐
6. chaffeur ☐
7. dissapointment ☐
8. disruption ☐
9. divisable ☐
10. fluourescent ☐
11. gyrascope ☐
12. irrisistible ☐
13. ilegall ☐
14. lyric ☐
15. mistrustfull ☐
16. misguide ☐
17. precisely ☐
18. placque ☐
19. senseably ☐
20. tympany ☐
21. unperceivied ☐
22. variable ☐

SCORE _______ /22

TEST 12.10

1. achievement ☐
2. bouquet ☐
3. chivalrous ☐
4. cryptic ☐
5. consideribly ☐
6. charade ☐
7. dammage ☐
8. defieciency ☐
9. disbelievingly ☐
10. disposess ☐
11. environmentally ☐
12. flimsily ☐
13. historicly ☐
14. ireversible ☐
15. literally ☐
16. misspelled ☐
17. noticeably ☐
18. orchid ☐
19. programable ☐
20. psychye ☐
21. recipies ☐
22. separately ☐

SCORE ______ /22

TEST 12.11

1. adolescent ☐
2. bronchittis ☐
3. catologue ☐
4. completely ☐
5. crescent ☐
6. debatible ☐
7. democratically ☐
8. discontinueing ☐
9. disenchanted ☐
10. dissatissfied ☐
11. ecquestrian ☐
12. grotesque ☐
13. hoarsley ☐
14. ilegitimate ☐
15. mistreatment ☐
16. opaque ☐
17. pistacchio ☐
18. purchase ☐
19. queazy ☐
20. reversable ☐
21. synddicate ☐
22. suggestable ☐

SCORE ______ /22

TEST 12.12

1. abominabley ☐
2. begrudgingly ☐
3. chrysanthmums ☐
4. concietedness ☐
5. crèeche ☐
6. deppendably ☐
7. disadvantadge ☐
8. disagreable ☐
9. discourteous ☐
10. disembarcked ☐
11. disimilarity ☐
12. effevescent ☐
13. gymkana ☐
14. hierarchical ☐
15. isosceles ☐
16. ill-legible ☐
17. matyr ☐
18. missapprehension ☐
19. naiively ☐
20. omniescient ☐
21. photosynethesis ☐
22. questionable ☐

SCORE ______ /22

> **Complete the following sentences by adding either the prefix <u>im-</u> or <u>in-</u> to each of the given words to form a word that has the OPPOSITE meaning to the given word.**
>
> **_Example:_ _The opposite of perfect is _________ ._**
>   _The opposite of perfect is <u>imperfect</u>._

1. The opposite of **mature** is _____________________ .

2. The opposite of **attentive** is _____________________ .

3. The opposite of **correct** is _____________________ .

4. The opposite of **balance** is _____________________ .

5. The opposite of **advisable** is _____________________ .

6. The opposite of **mortal** is _____________________ .

7. The opposite of **patient** is _____________________ .

8. The opposite of **definite** is _____________________ .

9. The opposite of **prudent** is _____________________ .

10. The opposite of **famous** is _____________________ .

11. The opposite of **adequate** is _____________________ .

12. The opposite of **practical** is _____________________ .

13. The opposite of **sufficient** is _____________________ .

14. The opposite of **precise** is _____________________ .

15. The opposite of **justice** is _____________________ .

16. The opposite of **valid** is _____________________ .

17. The opposite of **moral** is _____________________ .

18. The opposite of **edible** is _____________________ .

19. The opposite of **moveable** is _____________________ .

In each of the following, select the prefix that creates a correctly spelt word which sensibly completes each sentence.

Example: **Make sure you do not (in / re / im)pose on people's generosity.**
Make sure you do not (in / re / *im*)pose on people's generosity.

20. No decisions can be made until we (inter / re / in)view the results of the experiment.

21. It's surprising how many people choose to (inter / re / im)migrate each year.

22. Rewrite the following sentences as (in / re / im)direct speech.

23. It will cost a fortune to (im / in / re)novate that nineteenth-century building.

24. Kim only (in / im / re)plied that she would come; she never gave us a definite answer.

25. Our school has a yearly (inter / re / in)take of one hundred pupils.

26. Many doctors have (re / in / inter)jected the government's new plans for the NHS.

27. Luke missed the (inter / re / im)play of last week's Arsenal and Chelsea match.

28. The stubborn knight (in / re / inter)fused to take the old woman's advice.

29. Follow this road until it (inter / in / re)sects with Park Avenue, then turn left.

30. Once again, we have been (im / re / in)formed that the elevator is not working.

31. "These rare flowers," said the journalist, "have been (im / re / in)ported from China."

32. Please (im / re / inter)connect your computer to the Internet and try again.

33. We were (in / im / re)pelled by the stench of the week-old rubbish.

34. Mount Tringo, a volcano in the Pacific, has been (im / re / in)active for over fifty years.

35. This is only an (in / inter / im)mediate solution; we still need to find a permanent one.

36. You will (in / re / im)cur another fine if you don't return your library books tomorrow.

37. The local clinic has facilities for those with (in / re / im)paired hearing.

38. As Peter lies so frequently, I'm not (im / in / re)clined to believe any of his complaints.

> **Complete the following statements using the prefix <u>im-</u>, <u>in-</u>, <u>re-</u>, or <u>inter-</u>. Then write the correctly spelt word in the space provided.**
>
> ***Example:***   ___ + **work** ⇨ __________
>
>   <u>re</u> + work ⇨ _rework_

39. ______ + national ⇨ ______________   55. ______ + destructible ⇨ ___________

40. ______ + decorate ⇨ ______________   56. ______ + personal ⇨ ______________

41. ______ + prove ⇨ ______________   57. ______ + mission ⇨ ______________

42. ______ + humane ⇨ ______________   58. ______ + capable ⇨ ______________

43. ______ + accurate ⇨ ______________   59. ______ + dignity ⇨ ______________

44. ______ + act ⇨ ______________   60. ______ + boot ⇨ ______________

45. ______ + claim ⇨ ______________   61. ______ + mobile ⇨ ______________

46. ______ + change ⇨ ______________   62. ______ + compatible ⇨ ___________

47. ______ + polite ⇨ ______________   63. ______ + twine ⇨ ______________

48. ______ + acquaint ⇨ ______________   64. ______ + generate ⇨ ______________

49. ______ + formal ⇨ ______________   65. ______ + separable ⇨ ___________

50. ______ + city ⇨ ______________   66. ______ + plausible ⇨ ______________

51. ______ + plant ⇨ ______________   67. ______ + material ⇨ ______________

52. ______ + library ⇨ ______________   68. ______ + galactic ⇨ ______________

53. ______ + fund ⇨ ______________   69. ______ + conclusive ⇨ ___________

54. ______ + consider ⇨ ______________   70. ______ + pertinent ⇨ ___________

In each of the following groups, three words end with the same sound. Identify the one word that does NOT sound the same as the others and write it in the space provided.

Example: **wait plait freight slate**   ______________

           wait plait freight slate   *plait*

1. rough   tough   ruff   cough   ______________________

2. doubt   drought   route   clout   ______________________

3. foe   tow   dough   vow   ______________________

4. trout   bought   wart   fraught   ______________________

5. thorough   duller   cower   colour   ______________________

6. trough   plough   bough   thou   ______________________

7. ewe   true   through   rogue   ______________________

8. thought   naught   draught   wrought   ______________________

9. hour   flower   borough   sour   ______________________

10. nought   caught   quart   chart   ______________________

11. south   sought   sort   fort   ______________________

12. fought   pout   taut   taught   ______________________

13. throughout   nowt   gout   throat   ______________________

14. bellow   furlough   sallow   allow   ______________________

15. bout   ought   thwart   distraught   ______________________

16. although   below   hiccough   woe   ______________________

Read each sentence carefully. Then complete the statements beneath each sentence. Write your answers in the spaces provided.

Example: *You must always use knives carefully.*
The word with the silent letter is <u>knives</u> *. The silent letter is* <u>k</u> *.*

1. "I have no doubts at all that everything will work out in the end!" said Janet.
   The word with the silent letter is ___________________. The silent letter is ______.

2. On Friday, Poppy slipped on the icy pavement and pulled a muscle in her leg.
   The word with the silent letter is ___________________. The silent letter is ______.

3. We aren't sure if the island of Atlantis actually existed or if it is just a myth.
   The word with the silent letter is ___________________. The silent letter is ______.

4. Carol always has three digestive biscuits with her cup of coffee in the afternoon.
   The word with the silent letter is ___________________. The silent letter is ______.

5. "I think the minted lamb chops with chips is the best dish on the menu," Ash said.
   The word with the silent letter is ___________________. The silent letter is ______.

6. As we arrived at the mansion, we noticed that several vehicles were parked outside.
   The word with the silent letter is ___________________. The silent letter is ______.

7. "You have no business snooping about in my room," Gina said to her brother angrily.
   The word with the silent letter is ___________________. The silent letter is ______.

8. "The time has come," announced the King of the Elves solemnly, "for us to leave Avalon."
   The word with the silent letter is ___________________. The silent letter is ______.

9. Harry succumbed to temptation and treated himself to an expensive holiday.
   The word with the silent letter is ___________________. The silent letter is ______.

10. I have just discovered that the national emblem of Scotland is the thistle.
    The word with the silent letter is ___________________. The silent letter is ______.

11. We can't stand the cologne that our grandmother uses; it smells positively awful!
    The word with the silent letter is ___________________. The silent letter is ______.

One word in each of the following sentences is missing a letter string. Read the sentence carefully to work out what the word is. Then, fill in the missing letters so that the word is spelt correctly. Watch out for silent letters!

Example: *Every morning, Ashish brushes his teeth and c_______s his hair.*
Every morning, Ashish brushes his teeth and <u>c</u>om<u>b</u>s his hair.

12. The young children were f_______________d by the colourful fish in the aquarium.

13. The a_______________t discovered the tomb of an ancient Egyptian princess in Thebes.

14. Bill's dog is a terrible n_______________e; it keeps burying bones in my back garden.

15. People q_______________d for over two hours to get into the popular shopping mall.

16. The Old Man of the Sea's face was very w_______________d, but he had kindly eyes.

17. The police dogs picked up the robber's s_______________t very easily.

18. A w_______________k of a treasure ship that sank in the Adriatic has been found.

19. The word 'chilly' r_______________s with the word 'silly'.

20. "Would you like your r_______________t?" the pleasant cashier asked me.

21. The fox pricked up its ears; something was r_______________g in the nearby bushes.

22. "All c_______________s must be handled with great care," said our science teacher.

23. There are no g_______________s that our plan will work, but we must try something!

24. Realising his prisoners had escaped, the giant g_______________d his teeth angrily.

25. Last year, poor Paolo caught p_______________a and was very ill indeed.

26. As he was in d_______________e, nobody recognised the famous film star.

27. I owe a huge d_______________t of gratitude to everyone who has supported me.

28. The young shepherd put some bread and cheese in his k_______________k and set off.

29. Local residents are c_______________g very hard for their library to stay open.

30. C_______________s, like those in Rome, are ancient underground cemeteries.

In each of the following, add as many of the word endings as possible in the **Word Endings Bank** to each of the given root words, making any necessary changes. **Write your answers in the boxes provided. Be careful: some root words will accept more word endings than others.**

Example:

urge
urgent
urgency

WORD ENDINGS BANK

-ant   **-ance**   **-ancy**   **-ent**   **-ence**   **-ency**

1. observe

2. differ

3. hinder

4. obey

5. hesitate

6. expect

7. reside

8. assist

9. correspond

10. suffice

11. survey

12. depend

Each of the following sentences contains ONE spelling mistake. Find the misspelt word and write the correct spelling on the line beneath the sentence.

Example: *The soothing fragrence of freshly-baked bread filled the air.*

fragrance

13. There has been a noticeable increment in the efficiency of our staff this year.

____

14. That seemingly innocent-looking plant contains a poisonous substence.

____

15. I believe in the fundamental decency and tolerence of humanity.

____

16. The supporters of the independant candidate were confident she would win the vote.

____

17. The frequency of the customer's insistant demands was tiresome.

____

18. "Your persistent disobedeience is very disappointing," said the teacher.

____

19. I must have your assurances that you will not be negligient in this matter.

____

20. The recipiant of this writer's award must possess both eloquence and brilliance.

____

21. The defiant endurance and resiliance of the rebel leader was extremely impressive.

____

22. A key componant of a coherent, competent piece of writing is good structure.

____

23. The malevolent judge showed no leniance in the extended sentences that he passed.

____

24. The extent of his inefficiency was apparent to us all, as was his incompetency.

____

For each of the following, select the word that correctly completes the sentence.

**Example:**   **Sheila always has (one / won) biscuit with her cup of tea.**
Sheila always has (<u>one</u> / won) biscuit with her cup of tea.

1. There was nothing they could do to (altar / alter) the headmaster's decision.

2. It is usually a good idea to (draught / draft) your ideas before beginning your essay.

3. My grandmother always used to say, "(Practice / Practise) makes perfect."

4. Oedipus correctly (guest / guessed) the answer to the Sphinx's riddle.

5. A day of national (morning / mourning) has been declared.

6. (Steel / Steal) is an alloy that is a mixture of iron and other metals.

7. Do you have any idea (who's / whose) in charge of this department?

8. Julian always (bruise / brews) a pot of peppermint tea for us whenever we visit him.

9. The wounded (heart / hart) was surrounded by the huntsmen's dogs.

10. "I'm afraid I cannot (accept / except) this gift; it's far too expensive," said Pia firmly.

11. The (principle / principal) cause of this problem is a lack of organisation.

12. There is a very good (stationery / stationary) shop on St Peter's Avenue.

13. The brave general (led / lead) his troops into battle.

14. The spoilt child began to (ball / bawl) when its mother took its toys away.

15. The claim that The (Great / Grate) Wall of China can be seen from the moon is untrue.

16. I am always (wary / weary) of things that seem too good to be true.

17. The mad scientist tried to (device / devise) a time-travelling machine.

18. "This TV (cereal / serial) is one of the worst that I've seen in ages!" said the reviewer.

19. The Prime Minister refused to (ascent / assent) to the plan.

20. "I would like to make one (further / farther) suggestion," Micha said.

21. Surprisingly, the (bridal / bridle) party arrived at the church on time.

22. As we have been working hard, I believe we would all (prophet / profit) from a break.

23. The debate has had no (affect / effect) whatsoever on people's views.

24. The (herd / heard) of buffalo moved slowly across the prairie.

25. "What are we having for (desert / dessert)?" asked Phil.

26. The new carpet in the living room (compliments / complements) the sofa nicely.

27. Fresh fruit and vegetables are to be found in the last (aisle / isle).

28. "We must (proceed / precede) quietly so as not to wake the dragon," whispered Sinbad.

29. The school is (lightning / lightening) our classrooms by painting them white.

30. "You should not (meddle / medal) with magic you don't understand," warned Merlin.

31. In some countries, you need a special (license / licence) to own a dog.

32. As the bus went (past / passed), a crowd of tourists waved at us.

33. The following instructions should be read (aloud / allowed) to the students.

34. There was a great deal of (descent / dissent) among the billionaire's heirs.

35. "I (prophecy / prophesy) that you will become king," the strange woman told the knight.

36. As the fog was so dense, Sherlock Holmes (missed / mist) a crucial clue.

37. The forecaster doesn't know (weather / whether) it will rain tomorrow or not.

38. "That is the worst piece of (advice / advise) anyone has given me," snorted Ivy.

39. The (currant / current) economic situation in Europe is very worrying.

40. Being a nurse requires a great deal of (patients / patience).

41. The distraught mother (wrung / rung) her hands in despair.

See how well you remember the correct spellings of the words in Units 13-17! In all of the following tests, show whether each word is correct or incorrect.

**Examples:**   *hello*   ☑

                 wellcome   ☒

TEST 18.1	TEST 18.2	TEST 18.3
1. allow ☐	1. assistence ☐	1. acsent ☐
2. boute ☐	2. although ☐	2. biscuits ☐
3. chart ☐	3. cereial ☐	3. colour ☐
4. device ☐	4. chemicles ☐	4. confident ☐
5. differrent ☐	5. deppendence ☐	5. descency ☐
6. doubt ☐	6. disguize ☐	6. draught ☐
7. exept ☐	7. duller ☐	7. foughted ☐
8. flower ☐	8. hesitent ☐	8. imigrate ☐
9. imaterial ☐	9. immediate ☐	9. imbalance ☐
10. impacient ☐	10. inpersonal ☐	10. implied ☐
11. imported ☐	11. incapabable ☐	11. indefinate ☐
12. inactive ☐	12. in-formal ☐	12. inhumain ☐
13. ineffiecency ☐	13. indignity ☐	13. inconclusive ☐
14. incorrect ☐	14. intresects ☐	14. interview ☐
15. international ☐	15. lamb ☐	15. invallid ☐
16. island ☐	16. mournning ☐	16. lienience ☐
17. obediant ☐	17. noughty ☐	17. muscel ☐
18. practice ☐	18. poute ☐	18. principel ☐
19. resedency ☐	19. rogue ☐	19. queued ☐
20. south ☐	20. seriel ☐	20. stationiery ☐

| SCORE ______ /20 | SCORE ______ /20 | SCORE ______ /20 |

TEST 18.4	TEST 18.5	TEST 18.6
1. allowed	1. apparrent	1. advice
2. bought	2. bellow	2. accept
3. competance	3. collogne	3. curant
4. discent	4. caughten	4. cower
5. differance	5. devise	5. dett
6. dough	6. facsinated	6. expectance
7. grate	7. hinderance	7. hicough
8. immoral	8. immature	8. improve
9. inpolite	9. inpractical	9. inmobile
10. inedibble	10. infamous	10. injustice
11. injected	11. innovate	11. inseparible
12. incompetence	12. lisence	12. interlibary
13. intercity	13. medle	13. lightning
14. missed	14. quart	14. naught
15. nuiscance	15. reboot	15. persistant
16. proceede	16. repaired	16. reclaim
17. prophecy	17. refund	17. review
18. reaquaint	18. retake	18. replay
19. resident	19. scent	19. rung
20. sallow	20. taught	20. sufficient
21. sour	21. wether	21. solemly
22. thurough	22. wrinckled	22. rought

SCORE _______ /22   SCORE _______ /22   SCORE _______ /22

TEST 18.7

1. assistent ☐
2. brews ☐
3. complaments ☐
4. cought ☐
5. dependancy ☐
6. gnashed ☐
7. impairred ☐
8. innocent ☐
9. inacurrate ☐
10. incremente ☐
11. observence ☐
12. profit ☐
13. patience ☐
14. redecorate ☐
15. reconnect ☐
16. rhyhms ☐
17. stationary ☐
18. saught ☐
19. thissle ☐
20. thoughted ☐
21. wart ☐
22. woe ☐

SCORE ______ /22

TEST 18.8

1. alltar ☐
2. component ☐
3. clout ☐
4. deffiant ☐
5. endurancy ☐
6. frought ☐
7. frequency ☐
8. impelled ☐
9. insuffiscient ☐
10. inadvisable ☐
11. intermission ☐
12. negligient ☐
13. reformed ☐
14. redirect ☐
15. recepit ☐
16. rustleing ☐
17. substants ☐
18. through ☐
19. trout ☐
20. weary ☐
21. wrek ☐
22. vehicels ☐

SCORE ______ /22

TEST 18.9

1. assent ☐
2. below ☐
3. correspondant ☐
4. doubts ☐
5. futher ☐
6. implant ☐
7. intake ☐
8. inclined ☐
9. intertwine ☐
10. malevolant ☐
11. ought ☐
12. obedience ☐
13. prophesy ☐
14. reggenerate ☐
15. refused ☐
16. reconsider ☐
17. rough ☐
18. throut ☐
19. tough ☐
20. tolerence ☐
21. wheather ☐
22. wrung ☐

SCORE ______ /22

TEST 18.10

1. advise ☐
2. archeologist ☐
3. bawl ☐
4. compliament ☐
5. coherant ☐
6. dessent ☐
7. disobedience ☐
8. efficience ☐
9. farther ☐
10. gout ☐
11. hesitance ☐
12. immortal ☐
13. inpertinent ☐
14. inadecquate ☐
15. independent ☐
16. intermediate ☐
17. lisense ☐
18. prinsiple ☐
19. residence ☐
20. reported ☐
21. sufficiancy ☐
22. through-out ☐

SCORE ______ /22

TEST 18.11

1. alloud ☐
2. bridel ☐
3. business ☐
4. current ☐
5. catacoombs ☐
6. dependent ☐
7. drought ☐
8. expectent ☐
9. foe ☐
10. immovible ☐
11. imprescise ☐
12. incompatible ☐
13. informed ☐
14. intergalactic ☐
15. meddel ☐
16. observent ☐
17. preceede ☐
18. prophit ☐
19. repelled ☐
20. recurr ☐
21. surveillence ☐
22. taut ☐

SCORE ______ /22

TEST 18.12

1. assurrances ☐
2. burrough ☐
3. correspondance ☐
4. campaining ☐
5. distraught ☐
6. eloquents ☐
7. furrlough ☐
8. guarantees ☐
9. implausable ☐
10. inprudent ☐
11. indestructable ☐
12. inattentive ☐
13. interjected ☐
14. napsack ☐
15. lightenning ☐
16. patients ☐
17. pnuemonia ☐
18. resillience ☐
19. recipiant ☐
20. route ☐
21. sucumbed ☐
22. thwart ☐

SCORE ______ /22

For each of the following, select the one prefix from the choices given that correctly completes the given word.

Example: *"The phone that you sold me yesterday is ___standard," complained Mr Brown.*

  ☐ *super*   ☐ *anti*   ■ *sub*   ☐ *sub-*

1. All of these items can be bought at your local ___market.

  ☐ anti   ☐ sub   ☐ auto   ☐ super

2. The local council is forming a special ___committee to investigate this matter.

  ☐ sub-   ☐ sub   ☐ super   ☐ super-

3. "You need to put some ___septic on that wound," the nurse told Emma.

  ☐ auto   ☐ super   ☐ sub   ☐ anti

4. Scientists have divided the animal kingdom into numerous ___categories.

  ☐ sub   ☐ auto-   ☐ anti-   ☐ super

5. The teenage fans went wild when their favourite ___stars emerged from their limos.

  ☐ auto   ☐ anti   ☐ super   ☐ sub

6. I would love to own an ___graph of a famous novelist.

  ☐ super   ☐ auto   ☐ sub   ☐ anti

7. Lola's memories of her childhood were buried deep in her ___conscious.

  ☐ anti   ☐ auto   ☐ super   ☐ sub

8. After all the excitement of the holidays, going back to work was an ___climax.

  ☐ sub-   ☐ super-   ☐ anti-   ☐ anti

9. The HMS Seahorse was a ___marine that was sunk during World War II.

  ☐ super   ☐ anti   ☐ sub   ☐ auto-

10. Sophie enjoys reading ___biographies of famous actors.

  ☐ auto   ☐ auto-   ☐ super   ☐ anti-

In each of the following, use an appropriate prefix from the Prefix Bank with the root word supplied in brackets to create a correctly spelt new word that sensibly completes each sentence. Remember to use hyphens where necessary.

Example: *Many heroes in myths from around the world possess __________. (powers)*
Many heroes in myths from around the world possess <u>superpowers</u>*. (powers)*

PREFIX BANK

sub- super- anti- auto-

11. To switch the oven off, you must turn this knob ____________________. (clockwise)

12. The wyvern is a ________________ creature that is part dragon, part griffin. (natural)

13. "Remember to give your article a ________________," our teacher reminded us. (title)

14. According to ancient Greek myths, Hercules, had ______________ strength. (human)

15. What do you get if you ________________ 634 from 1,597? (tract)

16. Mr Howard has had his car fitted with an ________________device. (theft)

17. Tom believes he's a ______________; he's always trying to do the impossible. (man)

18. The town was almost completely ________________ by the flood. (merged)

19. In the past, people used to call cars ________________. (mobiles)

20. I think I can fix that broken vase with some ________________. (glue)

21. An ________________ is a type of medicine used to treat certain diseases. (biotic)

22. The photographer has ________________ an image over the original one. (imposed)

23. The teacher ________________ the class into three teams of ten. (divided)

24. ________________ is the North American word for an underground railway. (way)

25. The ________________ of the thriller was 'Be Very Afraid!'. (heading)

26. Every year, ________________ become faster and faster. (computers)

27. Hilda works as a ________________ at our local newspaper. (editor)

Complete the following tables with the correctly spelt plural form of each given word.

Example:	Singular	Plural
	dog	dogs

SINGULAR	PLURAL
1. girl	
2. knave	
3. tomato	
4. celebration	
5. woman	
6. mouse	
7. ibis	
8. anniversary	
9. foot	
10. man	
11. sheep	
12. privilege	
13. rhythm	
14. ox	
15. igloo	
16. child	
17. tooth	

SINGULAR	PLURAL
18. goose	
19. distillery	
20. attendee	
21. fox	
22. this	
23. miniature	
24. wife	
25. cactus	
26. liability	
27. louse	
28. volcano	
29. allegory	
30. loaf	
31. crisis	
32. deer	
33. that	
34. phenomenon	

> **For each of the following, underline the one correct spelling from the choices given in brackets.**
>
> ***Example:*** **The (flower's flowers flowers' flowers's) bobbed gently in the summer breeze.**
> The (flower's <u>flowers</u> flowers' flowers's) bobbed gently in the summer breeze.

35. The (childrens childrens' children's childrenes) laughter filled the air.

36. Many of the (soldierses' soldiers soldiers's soldiers') wounds never healed properly.

37. The (fish's fishes fishes' fishes's) were all covered with fluorescent scales.

38. Miriam has broken her father's (glasses glassess glasses's glasses') again.

39. Tara's new (shoes shoe's shoeses shoes') heels are extremely thin and high.

40. We will always have (controversies' controversys controversies controversie's).

41. The fans threw their (scarve's scarves scarves' scarves's) into the air in celebration.

42. The (amateurs amateures amateur's amateurs') drama club is held on Mondays.

43. The (firemen firemans' firemen's firemens's) bravery was astonishing.

44. My favourite biscuits are triple chocolate-chip (cookies cookys cooky's cookieses).

45. This device can't pick up those (radio's radioes radioes' radios') signals.

46. The (Peopleses Peoples' People's Peopleses') Republic of China is in Asia.

47. The White (Cliff's Cliffes Cliffes's Cliffs) of Dover are a world-famous landmark.

48. Various kinds of mushrooms are (funguses' fungis fungi fungus's) that are edible.

49. Sherine dislikes both (avocados avocadoes avocadoes' avocados') and guavas.

50. Turn to the back of the book for all the (quizzes quizes quizz's quizzes') solutions.

51. Various deserts all over the world possess stunning (oasis' oasises oases oaseses).

52. The (puppies puppys puppy's puppies') tails wagged excitedly when Gill came in.

53. There has been a (series serie serie's serieses) of complaints made.

54. The ancient Egyptians greatly feared (hippopotamii hippopotamuses hippopotamis hippopotamuses').

For each of the following, add an appropriate suffix to the root word supplied in brackets to complete the sentence in the most sensible way. Write the correctly spelt word in the space provided.

Example: *"Paul is doing really well!" said his sister excitedly. "It looks as though he is ________!" (win)*

"Paul is doing really well!" said his sister excitedly. "It looks as though he is <u>winning</u>!" (win)

1. Although Tom is just a ________________________, he is learning very quickly. (begin)

2. The estate employs a _______________________ to look after the grounds. (garden)

3. Our history teacher is an excellent ________________________. (communicate)

4. I have ______________________ all the chemistry I learned at school. (forget)

5. They have placed a ______________________ on imports from Russia. (limit)

6. That car is ______________________ with a Tom Tom sat nav. (equip)

7. When I was little, I got very badly _____________________ one summer. (sunburn)

8. The billionaire owned a highly successful ________________________ company. (ship)

9. We have no idea why this glitch keeps ______________________. (occur)

10. My parents keep _____________________ me to study harder. (nag)

11. All the _____________________ for the school fair have been completed. (prepare)

12. The accused was ______________________ by the court. (acquit)

13. My father is a very talented chemical ________________________. (engine)

14. Penny spent ages ______________________ with the shopkeeper. (bargain)

15. Many areas in the country suffer from ______________________. (overpopulate)

16. The last ______________________ we had was called Marnie. (babysit)

17. Keith has ______________________ all of the responsibility for this. (shoulder)

18. Neil sat in the corner and gently ______________________ his guitar. (strum)

19. An aircraft ______________________ is a warship from which planes take off. (carry)

> For each of the following, select the one letter string that correctly completes the given word. Each word has been defined to help you.
>
> *Example:* P______T *(adj.): nice*
>
> A.   LESAN   (B.)   LEASAN   C.   LEASSAN   D.   LEASEN

20. A______D (v.): gave a person a place to stay
    A.   COMODATE   B.   COMMADATE   C.   CCOMMODATE   D.   CCOMMADATTE

21. I______G (v.): taking steps to try to prevent something bad from happening
    A.   NSURIN   B.   NSURRIN   C.   NSSURIN   D.   NSSURRIN

22. F______D (v.): shaped or designed something a particular way
    A.   ORMATE   B.   ORMMATTE   C.   ORMMATE   D.   ORMATTE

23. E______G (v.): giving out (sound, light, etc.)
    A.   MITIN   B.   MMITIN   C.   MITTIN   D.   MMITTIN

24. U______D (v.): lacked concentration or attention
    A.   NFFOCUSE   B.   NFOCUSE   C.   NFOCCUSSE   D.   NFOCCUSE

25. E______T (n.): a feeling of self-conscious awkwardness
    A.   MMBARASMEN   B.   MBARASMEN   C.   MBARASSMEN   D.   MBARRASSMEN

26. D______T (n.): a result or consequence
    A.   EVELOPPMEN   B.   EVELOPMEN   C.   EVELLOPMEN   D.   EVALOPMEN

27. E______R (n.): a person who listens secretly to a private conversation
    A.   VESDROPPE   B.   VESDROPE   C.   AVESDDROPE   D.   AVESDROPPE

28. P______D (v.): said or uttered words
    A.   RONOUNCE   B.   RONNOUNCE   C.   RONOUNNCE   D.   RONUNCE

29. E______D (v.): described something as better than it really was
    A.   XAGERATE   B.   XAGERRATE   C.   XAGGERATE   D.   XAGGARATE

In each of the following groups, **THREE** of the four words have been **MISSPELT. Complete the statements in the boxes to show which ONE word is CORRECTLY spelt and how the THREE remaining words SHOULD be spelt.**

Example: *tabel, chair, carppet, miror*

> **The one word that is spelt correctly is** chair.

> **The three remaining words should be spelt** table, carpet, mirror.

1. conferrence, deferral, diffrence, sufferred

> The one word that is spelt correctly is

> The three remaining words should be spelt

2. offered, infered, surffing, referance

> The one word that is spelt correctly is

> The three remaining words should be spelt

3. referal, preference, differring, confered

> The one word that is spelt correctly is

> The three remaining words should be spelt

4. referrendum, transferance, pilferring, refereed

> The one word that is spelt correctly is

> The three remaining words should be spelt

In each of the following, you are given the definition of a word. Select the one correct spelling of the word that is being defined from the choices given.

Example: Choice

    A. opcion   B. opption   C. opsion   (D.) option

5. A willingness to respect the wishes of other people
    A. defferrence   B. deference   C. deferrence   D. defference

6. Discussing or consulting together
    A. conferring   B. confering   C. conffering   D. confferring

7. Put something off until a later time
    A. defered   B. deffered   C. deferred   D. defferred

8. Stating one's willingness to do something
    A. ofering   B. offerring   C. oferring   D. offering

9. A judgement or conclusion based on facts
    A. inference   B. inferrence   C. infferrence   D. infference

10. Stole
    A. pilffered   B. pilfered   C. pilferred   D. pilfferred

11. Distress or pain
    A. sufferring   B. suferring   C. suffering   D. sufering

12. A person who stands or lies on a narrow board and tries to ride waves to the shore
    A. surfer   B. surrfer   C. surffer   D. surferer

13. Liked one thing more than another
    A. prefferred   B. preffered   C. prefered   D. preferred

14. To meddle in something that is not one's business
    A. interferre   B. interfere   C. interfferre   D. interffere

---

> Add the word ending **-tion**, **-sion**, **-ssion**, or **-cian** to each given root word to complete every statement. Make any necessary changes, then write the correctly spelt word in the space provided.
>
> **_Example:_** _delete +_ ___ ⇨ __________
>
> _delete + tion_ ⇨ _deletion_

1.   music + _____ ⇨ ______________

2.   commit + _____ ⇨ ______________

3.   decide + _____ ⇨ ______________

4.   educate + _____ ⇨ ______________

5.   discuss + _____ ⇨ ______________

6.   adopt + _____ ⇨ ______________

7.   include + _____ ⇨ ______________

8.   operate + _____ ⇨ ______________

9.   suggest + _____ ⇨ ______________

10. electric + _____ ⇨ ______________

11. predict + _____ ⇨ ______________

12. express + _____ ⇨ ______________

13. submit + _____ ⇨ ______________

14. elect + _____ ⇨ ______________

15. promote + _____ ⇨ ______________

16. divide + _____ ⇨ ______________

17. comprehend + _____ ⇨ ___________

18. attend + _____ ⇨ ______________

19. compress + _____ ⇨ ______________

20. insert + _____ ⇨ ______________

21. diffuse + _____ ⇨ ______________

22. omit + _____ ⇨ ______________

23. distort + _____ ⇨ ______________

24. suspend + _____ ⇨ ______________

25. profess + _____ ⇨ ______________

26. graduate + _____ ⇨ ______________

27. project + _____ ⇨ ______________

28. devote + _____ ⇨ ______________

29. contract + _____ ⇨ ______________

30. clinic + _____ ⇨ ______________

31. prevent + _____ ⇨ ______________

32. transmit + _____ ⇨ ______________

In each of the following, add the word ending **-tion**, **-sion**, **-ssion**, or **-cian** to each root word given in brackets. Make any necessary changes, then use the correctly spelt word to complete the sentence.

Example: _________ *films now cost huge sums of money. (act)*
         Action films now cost huge sums of money. (act)

33. Please submit an ___________________________________ with your project. (illustrate)

34. Ali wants to become an ___________________________ when he grows up. (optic)

35. I think we made a good ___________________________ at the meeting. (impress)

36. Levels of ___________________________ have reached a record high. (pollute)

37. The criminal refused to make an ___________________________ of guilt. (admit)

38. The new curriculum has caused much ___________________________. (confuse)

39. I have a ___________________________ to make; I've broken your TV. (confess)

40. Sally gave no ___________________________ that anything was wrong. (indicate)

41. Mrs Tully was prepared to make an ___________________________ for us. (except)

42. The teacher has given us ___________________________ to leave early. (permit)

43. Ian collapsed on the sofa in utter ___________________________. (exhaust)

44. There has been a large ___________________________ at a shoe factory. (explode)

45. A ___________________________ needs to be very good with numbers. (statistic)

46. "My ___________________________ is utterly honourable," swore Ed. (intend)

47. The hotel offers ___________________________ for large families. (accommodate)

48. The stomach is responsible for food ___________________________. (digest)

49. "I apologise for the ___________________________," said Mabel. (intrude)

50. The cowardly soldier was found guilty of ___________________________. (desert)

51. The ___________________________ of greenhouse gases must be curbed. (emit)

See how well you remember the correct spellings of the words in Units 19-23! In all of the following tests, show whether each word is correct or incorrect.

Examples: _hello_   ☑

                 wellcome   ☒

TEST 24.1

1. adoption ☐
2. anticlockwise ☐
3. babysit ☐
4. cactus ☐
5. cactuses ☐
6. catagories ☐
7. child ☐
8. commitee ☐
9. differrence ☐
10. engine ☐
11. education ☐
12. fox ☐
13. garden ☐
14. iggloo ☐
15. loaves ☐
16. musician ☐
17. ocurr ☐
18. preperations ☐
19. quizzes' ☐
20. rythms ☐

TEST 24.2

1. autobiographes ☐
2. bargain ☐
3. carrier ☐
4. celebration ☐
5. conferrence ☐
6. deer ☐
7. divided ☐
8. desert ☐
9. descision ☐
10. forget ☐
11. fishes's ☐
12. girl ☐
13. gooses ☐
14. liability ☐
15. merged ☐
16. oxe ☐
17. privilige ☐
18. peoples's ☐
19. refferral ☐
20. sufferring ☐

TEST 24.3

1. aquitt ☐
2. allegry ☐
3. antitheft ☐
4. begin ☐
5. communnicate ☐
6. contractian ☐
7. defered ☐
8. distillary ☐
9. developpment ☐
10. electian ☐
11. foot ☐
12. glasseses ☐
13. impose ☐
14. knave ☐
15. limitation ☐
16. man ☐
17. pilfererd ☐
18. phenomemon ☐
19. sunburnned ☐
20. surfing ☐

SCORE ______ /20   **SCORE** ______ /20   **SCORE** ______ /20

TEST 24.4

1. accommadated ☐
2. antibiotic ☐
3. confussion ☐
4. cookies ☐
5. digestion ☐
6. discusssion ☐
7. equip ☐
8. electrician ☐
9. geeses ☐
10. illlustration ☐
11. ibis ☐
12. insertion ☐
13. minature ☐
14. offerred ☐
15. pollutian ☐
16. proffession ☐
17. shoulder ☐
18. suspention ☐
19. suggestian ☐
20. subway ☐
21. superman ☐
22. tomatoe ☐

SCORE _______ /22

TEST 24.5

1. aniversaries ☐
2. attendee ☐
3. confered ☐
4. childrens's ☐
5. commission ☐
6. deferance ☐
7. explosion ☐
8. girls ☐
9. iglooes ☐
10. men ☐
11. overpoppulate ☐
12. ommission ☐
13. prediction ☐
14. preferrence ☐
15. prefferred ☐
16. referrence ☐
17. refereed ☐
18. strum ☐
19. shiping ☐
20. subdivided ☐
21. subtract ☐
22. teeth ☐

SCORE _______ /22

TEST 24.6

1. attention ☐
2. childs' ☐
3. celebrations ☐
4. crisses ☐
5. deers ☐
6. division ☐
7. impression ☐
8. interferre ☐
9. limit ☐
10. nag ☐
11. projection ☐
12. pro-nounced ☐
13. soldier's ☐
14. serie's ☐
15. shoe's ☐
16. surfer ☐
17. sunburnt ☐
18. subcommitee ☐
19. subtitle ☐
20. superglue ☐
21. this ☐
22. unfoccused ☐

SCORE _______ /22

TEST 24.7

1. autograph ☐
2. bruise ☐
3. carry ☐
4. clockwise ☐
5. distortian ☐
6. expresion ☐
7. gardner ☐
8. knaves ☐
9. occurring ☐
10. operacion ☐
11. prepare ☐
12. prommotion ☐
13. radios' ☐
14. ship ☐
15. subcontious ☐
16. subcatagories ☐
17. superhuman ☐
18. septical ☐
19. statistic ☐
20. volcano ☐
21. whose's ☐
22. wife ☐

SCORE _______ /22

TEST 24.8

1. amatueurs ☐
2. begginner ☐
3. cliffes ☐
4. comprescion ☐
5. distileries ☐
6. exaggerrated ☐
7. indication ☐
8. inclusion ☐
9. lice ☐
10. mouse ☐
11. prevension ☐
12. sheep ☐
13. submission ☐
14. subheading ☐
15. subediter ☐
16. supermarket ☐
17. tooth ☐
18. these ☐
19. theif ☐
20. that ☐
21. trans-mission ☐
22. woman ☐

SCORE _______ /22

TEST 24.9

1. admission ☐
2. anticlimax ☐
3. communicater ☐
4. controvesies ☐
5. differring ☐
6. devotion ☐
7. emmitting ☐
8. engineer ☐
9. foxes ☐
10. feets ☐
11. graduation ☐
12. infered ☐
13. oasis ☐
14. permission ☐
15. privileges ☐
16. puppies's ☐
17. referendem ☐
18. sufferred ☐
19. submarine ☐
20. submerged ☐
21. superstars ☐
22. scarves ☐

SCORE _______ /22

TEST 24.10

1. allegaries ☐
2. anniversary ☐
3. avocadoes ☐
4. babysitter ☐
5. biographies ☐
6. crissis ☐
7. clinician ☐
8. defferral ☐
9. exceptian ☐
10. forggotten ☐
11. intrusion ☐
12. ibeses ☐
13. insuring ☐
14. loaf ☐
15. offerring ☐
16. optiscian ☐
17. oxen ☐
18. pilffering ☐
19. strumed ☐
20. supernatural ☐
21. those ☐
22. who's ☐

SCORE _______ /22

TEST 24.11

1. attendees ☐
2. automobiles ☐
3. bargainning ☐
4. confession ☐
5. children's ☐
6. dessertion ☐
7. exhuaustion ☐
8. equipped ☐
9. firemens' ☐
10. fungi ☐
11. intention ☐
12. liabilaties ☐
13. mice ☐
14. nagging ☐
15. oasses ☐
16. rhythem ☐
17. shouldered ☐
18. sheeps ☐
19. sunburn ☐
20. supercomputers ☐
21. tomatos ☐
22. volcanos ☐

SCORE _______ /22

TEST 24.12

1. accommodation ☐
2. acquited ☐
3. antisceptic ☐
4. confering ☐
5. comprehension ☐
6. difussion ☐
7. emission ☐
8. eaveasdropper ☐
9. embarrassment ☐
10. formated ☐
11. hippopotamuses ☐
12. inferrance ☐
13. louse ☐
14. miniatures ☐
15. overpopulation ☐
16. phenomena ☐
17. statistitician ☐
18. superimposed ☐
19. swott ☐
20. transferance ☐
21. women ☐
22. wives's ☐

SCORE _______ /22

In each of the following groups, two out of the five words do not begin with a prefix. Identify the two words that DO NOT START WITH A PREFIX.

Example: ____ *misjudge*
____ *extract*
__X__ *misery*
____ *enable*
__X__ *ready*

1. ____ supervision
____ interested
____ disarm
____ inaudible
____ superb

2. ____ antic
____ miscalculate
____ ill-advised
____ comet
____ expose

3. ____ contract
____ profess
____ discos
____ preen
____ extraordinary

4. ____ counter
____ unabridged
____ relative
____ reapplied
____ misfire

5. ____ increase
____ inner
____ ungrammatical
____ prologue
____ mister

6. ____ rebuilt
____ comma
____ discolour
____ coining
____ exclude

7. ____ pronoun
____ extraterrestrial
____ proudly
____ reedy
____ intervene

8. ____ imagine
____ autonomous
____ extract
____ dishonour
____ prowler

9. ____ unrepentant
____ antique
____ indistinct
____ unit
____ misplaced

10. ____ comely
____ convert
____ redeliver
____ condor
____ disown

11. ____ unresolvable
____ inequality
____ under
____ profiterole
____ proactive

12. ____ interred
____ disqualify
____ refill
____ exclaim
____ prodigy

13. ____ subcontinent
____ mistletoe
____ misremembered
____ external
____ interim

14. ____ inhibit
____ supersede
____ intern
____ properly
____ dissatisfied

15. ____ conical
____ insignificance
____ misdial
____ probing
____ extracurricular

Complete the following sentences by adding <u>im-</u>, <u>in-</u>, <u>ir-</u>, <u>dis-</u>, or <u>un-</u> to each of the given words to form a word that has the OPPOSITE meaning to the given word.

Example: *The opposite of perfect is _________ .*
            The opposite of perfect is imperfect .

16. The opposite of **perceptible** is ___________________ .

17. The opposite of **professional** is ___________________ .

18. The opposite of **accessible** is ___________________ .

19. The opposite of **advantage** is ___________________ .

20. The opposite of **compromising** is ___________________ .

21. The opposite of **considerate** is ___________________ .

22. The opposite of **characteristic** is ___________________ .

23. The opposite of **replaceable** is ___________________ .

24. The opposite of **belief** is ___________________ .

25. The opposite of **bearable** is ___________________ .

26. The opposite of **insured** is ___________________ .

27. The opposite of **animate** is ___________________ .

28. The opposite of **eligible** is ___________________ .

29. The opposite of **reconcilable** is ___________________ .

30. The opposite of **regarded** is ___________________ .

31. The opposite of **patriotic** is ___________________ .

32. The opposite of **appropriate** is ___________________ .

33. The opposite of **remarkable** is ___________________ .

34. The opposite of **effective** is ___________________ .

25 words are listed below. However, 10 of them are spelt incorrectly. Find the 10 incorrectly spelt words and write their correct spellings in the spaces provided.

uninterested	discontinued	disturbence	inacknowledged	improper
improbibly	irredeemable	interlaced	unfashionable	unrelevance
imprisonment	reallocated	subdivision	disdiagnose	misapprovingly
indrinkable	reevaluation	unadmissible	redoubling	unadvertised
subscript	uninvited	automatic	inpersonated	disoriented

1. _______________________   6. _______________________

2. _______________________   7. _______________________

3. _______________________   8. _______________________

4. _______________________   9. _______________________

5. _______________________   10. _______________________

ALL of the following words have been misspelt in at least one way. Write the correct spelling of each word in the space provided.

11. irepairable _______________   18. disaggrement _______________

12. undefinible _______________   19. unconsistence _______________

13. inexperiency _______________   20. misrespectfull _______________

14. incouragment _______________   21. reassurence _______________

15. proficience _______________   22. imprudance _______________

16. irreverant _______________   23. inemploymence _______________

17. misgoverment _______________   24. irretreivible _______________

Complete the following statements with the correctly spelt root words and appropriate word endings or suffixes.

Example: ___ + ___ ⇨ _boyish_

boy + _ish_ ⇨ _boyish_

25. __________ + _____ ⇨ jabbed

26. __________ + _____ ⇨ presidential

27. __________ + _____ ⇨ inducible

28. __________ + _____ ⇨ guidance

29. __________ + _____ ⇨ differed

30. __________ + _____ ⇨ irritation

31. __________ + _____ ⇨ urgency

32. __________ + _____ ⇨ obsession

33. __________ + _____ ⇨ chiselling

34. __________ + _____ ⇨ compliant

35. __________ + _____ ⇨ invention

36. __________ + _____ ⇨ hysterically

37. __________ + _____ ⇨ persuasion

38. __________ + _____ ⇨ rhetorician

39. __________ + _____ ⇨ ably

40. __________ + _____ ⇨ plodder

41. __________ + _____ ⇨ transferring

42. __________ + _____ ⇨ erosion

43. __________ + _____ ⇨ eerily

44. __________ + _____ ⇨ trekked

45. __________ + _____ ⇨ classifiable

46. __________ + _____ ⇨ idealistically

47. __________ + _____ ⇨ conscientious

48. __________ + _____ ⇨ transgression

49. __________ + _____ ⇨ absorbent

50. __________ + _____ ⇨ forensically

51. __________ + _____ ⇨ consequential

52. __________ + _____ ⇨ occupancy

53. __________ + _____ ⇨ coherence

54. __________ + _____ ⇨ flogging

55. __________ + _____ ⇨ completion

56. __________ + _____ ⇨ succession

Complete the following table with the correctly spelt singular or plural form of each given word.

Examples:

Singular	Plural
cat	cats
book	_books_

SINGULAR	PLURAL
1. mine	
2.	bosses
3.	thieves
4. chief	
5.	complexes
6. echo	
7.	bookworms
8. his	
9.	anchovies
10. alley	
11.	mattresses
12. puff	
13. rhinoceros	
14.	ourselves
15. handkerchief	
16. advice	

SINGULAR	PLURAL
17. giraffe	
18. moose	
19.	barracks
20.	lampshades
21.	matchsticks
22. commando	
23.	indices
24. belief	
25.	allies
26. torpedo	
27.	yours
28. confectionery	
29. offspring	
30.	axes
31. zero	
32. archipelago	

> **Each of the following sentences contains ONE spelling mistake. Find the misspelt word and write the correct spelling on the line beneath the sentence.**
>
> _Example:_   _Those girls and boys' are in my class._
>
>   _boys_ ____

33. At the zoo, we saw many animals including snakes, bisons, lions, tigers, and llamas.

____

34. The book contained lots of pictures and interesting informations about the planets.

____

35. The French and Italian ships' cargoes' of luxuries were unloaded at the docks.

____

36. The roof's of the cottages were covered with pretty red tiles that were sixty years old.

____

37. Ulalia gazed up at the beautiful spines lining the bookshelfs in the house's main hall.

____

38. The sound of the oboes's crescendos made the hairs on the back of my neck stand up.

____

39. The young apprentice over-boiled the chef's carrots, potatos, radishes, and leeks.

____

40. Susie loves the rhythms of tangos and calypsos, but she doesn't like those of waltzes'.

____

41. Flames and billowing smoke came out of the two dragons's large nostrils and mouths.

____

42. Mosquitos bites are usually harmless; sometimes, however, they can be dangerous.

____

43. Those dirty shoes over there are yours', as are the dirty clothes on the chairs.

____

44. The gnomes were responsible for the hoax's played on the fairies' children.

____

Use the clues given to help you work out what each gender word is. Then, fill in the missing letters of each word so that it is spelt correctly.

Example: *The word for a female horse is* m _ _ _.
            The word for a female horse is m <u>a</u> <u>r</u> <u>e</u>.

1. The word for a male duck is **d** ___ ___ ___ ___.

2. The word for a female duck is **d** ___ ___ ___.

3. The word for a male chicken is **r** ___ ___ ___ ___ ___ ___.

4. The word for a female chicken is **h** ___ ___.

5. The word for a male goose is **g** ___ ___ ___ ___ ___.

6. The word for a female goose is **g** ___ ___ ___ ___.

7. The word for a male pig is **b** ___ ___ ___.

8. The word for a female pig is **s** ___ ___.

9. The word for a male sheep is **r** ___ ___.

10. The word for a female sheep is **e** ___ ___.

11. The word for a male cat is **t** ___ ___.

12. The word for a female tiger is **t** ___ ___ ___ ___ ___ ___.

13. The word for a male bee is **d** ___ ___ ___ ___.

14. The word for a male deer is **s** ___ ___ ___.

15. The word for a female fox is **v** ___ ___ ___ ___.

16. The word for a female peacock is **p** ___ ___ ___ ___ ___.

17. The word for a male whale is **b** ___ ___ ___.

18. The word for a female whale is **c** ___ ___.

Complete the following tables with the correctly spelt missing gender form of each given word.

Examples:

MASCULINE	FEMININE
man	**woman**
king	_queen_

MASCULINE	FEMININE		MASCULINE	FEMININE
19. duke			35. earl	
20.	bride		36. headmaster	
21. heir			37. god	
22.	lady		38. emperor	
23.	shepherdess		39.	madam
24. son			40. actor	
25.	waitress		41.	dam
26. brother			42. sultan	
27. abbot			43.	witch
28. manservant			44.	widow
29.	heroine		45. monk	
30. steward			46. bachelor	
31. Mr			47. uncle	
32. lad			48. marquis	
33.	princess		49.	fiancée
34.	mistress		50.	nanny goat

For each of the following, select the word that correctly completes the sentence.

Example: **Sheila always has (one / won) biscuit with her cup of tea.**
Sheila always has (<u>one</u> / won) biscuit with her cup of tea.

1. Pablo and Gamal made a (pact / packed) to remain best friends, no matter what.

2. "I believe that finding a cure for this disease is (eminent / imminent)," said Dr Polly.

3. "Over there," said Ivy, pointing at a bench. "That's where (were / we're) sitting."

4. None of the men in the town responded to the Sheriff's call to (alms / arms).

5. At the (bazaar / bizarre), we found many strange and wonderful spices, silks, and trinkets.

6. "This quest will test the (metal / mettle) of all my knights," announced King Arthur.

7. For my (aural / oral) test tomorrow, I have to recite a sonnet by Shakespeare.

8. The author wrote an interesting (foreword / forward) for her new book.

9. You will need three (quartz / quarts) of milk for this recipe.

10. "Such suspense simply cannot be (born / borne)! I must know the answer!" wailed Di.

11. If those children are left unattended, they will (reek / wreak) havoc.

12. Jehan is a real (swot / swat); she studies all the time, even at weekends!

13. The flour in the packet that we bought was surprisingly (course / coarse).

14. The (troop / troupe) of monkeys we saw at the circus performed some amazing tricks.

15. One way to kill a vampire is to drive a wooden (steak / stake) through its heart.

16. Mr Deloney and Mr Swift will fight a (duel / dual) with pistols at dawn tomorrow.

17. The government has (sort / sought) to find a solution to this problem, but has failed.

18. The Americans and the Japanese fought several (naval / navel) battles in World War II.

19. The poor frog was (cast / caste) aside by the unfeeling princess.

20. Jeanette couldn't decide (wear / where) to hang her grandmother's coat.

21. Several countries are currently experiencing the horrors of (gorilla / guerrilla) warfare.

22. The (suite / sweet) at the hotel that we stayed in was beautifully decorated.

23. As the bell (told / tolled), all the villagers rushed out to see what was happening.

24. "All (hale / hail) mighty Caesar!" roared the crowds in the Colosseum.

25. I cannot stand spoilt children who (whine / wine) all the time.

26. Mr Lawrence (mowed / mode) his lawn last Saturday, but it still looks a mess.

27. The molten (lava / larva) rolled down the hillside in great fiery waves.

28. Furniture in the eighteenth century was often (guilt / gilt) with gold leaf.

29. That's not Cindy and Alex's car; (they're / their) car is parked in the next street.

30. The (lone / loan) wolf slunk through the forest, revelling in his solitude.

31. "I would not (council / counsel) such action," said the vizier to his sultan.

32. The police have closed the (borders / boarders) to prevent the criminals from escaping.

33. A great (hoard / horde) of trolls emerged out of the forest and attacked the city.

34. "This won't (lessen / lesson) your distress, but it should teach you something," said Ida.

35. "Have you seen the latest TV (ads / adds) for Christmas?" asked Will. "They're terrible!"

36. Georgio wished only to be a scholar, but the (Fêtes / Fates) had other plans for him.

37. Every day, Keira runs at least five (laps / lapse) around the park.

38. Please make sure your clothes are put on their (hangars / hangers).

39. When you have finished that orange, throw the (peel / peal) in the food recycling bin.

40. "Here. Have some of this fruit juice," said Fred. "It'll (whet / wet) your appetite."

41. My aunt lives on the thirtieth (storey / story) of a skyscraper in New York.

See how well you remember the correct spellings of the words in Units 25-29! In all of the following tests, show whether each word is correct or incorrect.

**Examples:**   hello   ☑

               wellcome   ☒

TEST 30.1

1. abbott ☐
2. bizzare ☐
3. complient ☐
4. cargoe's ☐
5. disadvantage ☐
6. discontinued ☐
7. emperess ☐
8. extraordinary ☐
9. fourward ☐
10. giraffes ☐
11. head-master ☐
12. idealistically ☐
13. imminnent ☐
14. increese ☐
15. inconsistant ☐
16. indicies ☐
17. jabbed ☐
18. manservant ☐
19. offsprings ☐
20. potatoes ☐

SCORE _______ /20

TEST 30.2

1. alms ☐
2. borne ☐
3. calypsoes ☐
4. disagreemant ☐
5. discolor ☐
6. droan ☐
7. exclaim ☐
8. handkerchieves ☐
9. improbably ☐
10. indistinct ☐
11. infomation ☐
12. inhibit ☐
13. interlaced ☐
14. lamma ☐
15. mattresses ☐
16. miscalculate ☐
17. oural ☐
18. pronoun ☐
19. quartes ☐
20. realloccated ☐

SCORE _______ /20

TEST 30.3

1. allies ☐
2. alleys ☐
3. bison ☐
4. consequencial ☐
5. clothes ☐
6. disbelief ☐
7. dutchess ☐
8. external ☐
9. hieress ☐
10. ill-adviced ☐
11. inperceptable ☐
12. inequality ☐
13. invention ☐
14. marquiss ☐
15. misdiagnose ☐
16. nostrils ☐
17. occuppancy ☐
18. puffs ☐
19. rebuilt ☐
20. redoubbling ☐

SCORE _______ /20

TEST 30.4

1. abley ☐
2. bookworms ☐
3. completetion ☐
4. comandoes ☐
5. disarm ☐
6. exclude ☐
7. eeriely ☐
8. gorrilla ☐
9. heroine ☐
10. inproper ☐
11. inaccessable ☐
12. inconsiderate ☐
13. mode ☐
14. misfire ☐
15. oboes ☐
16. pact ☐
17. reassurrence ☐
18. radishes ☐
19. barraks ☐
20. supervision ☐
21. theire ☐
22. uncharacteristic ☐

SCORE ______ /22

TEST 30.5

1. automatic ☐
2. abbess ☐
3. chiseling ☐
4. cottages ☐
5. dishonour ☐
6. echos ☐
7. fianncée ☐
8. gnomes ☐
9. inadmissable ☐
10. indefinable ☐
11. irreconcilible ☐
12. luxiuries ☐
13. misdial ☐
14. navell ☐
15. plodder ☐
16. redeliver ☐
17. refill ☐
18. spinister ☐
19. tangos ☐
20. undrinkable ☐
21. unensured ☐
22. vixen ☐

SCORE ______ /22

TEST 30.6

1. beliefs ☐
2. councel ☐
3. chefs ☐
4. disown ☐
5. disaprovingly ☐
6. extract ☐
7. gilt ☐
8. inpersonated ☐
9. inducible ☐
10. inexperience ☐
11. irredemeable ☐
12. mettle ☐
13. misplaced ☐
14. ourselfs ☐
15. proffess ☐
16. reevaluation ☐
17. rooster ☐
18. stake ☐
19. subscript ☐
20. tiles ☐
21. unproffesional ☐
22. urgence ☐

SCORE ______ /22

TEST 30.7

1. anchoves ☐
2. bookshelves ☐
3. course ☐
4. children ☐
5. disqualify ☐
6. gander ☐
7. hangars ☐
8. inanimate ☐
9. ineffective ☐
10. irrelevence ☐
11. irreverrent ☐
12. matchsticks ☐
13. proactive ☐
14. reapplied ☐
15. rythymes ☐
16. storey ☐
17. swat ☐
18. troup ☐
19. uninterrested ☐
20. unadvertised ☐
21. waiteress ☐
22. widower ☐

SCORE ______ /22

TEST 30.8

1. aural ☐
2. boarders ☐
3. contract ☐
4. complexes ☐
5. disregarded ☐
6. expose ☐
7. godess ☐
8. hoaxes ☐
9. imprisonmment ☐
10. inaproppriate ☐
11. inconsistancy ☐
12. irreparable ☐
13. misgovernment ☐
14. obssession ☐
15. persuasion ☐
16. sultan ☐
17. theyr'e ☐
18. thiefs ☐
19. uninvited ☐
20. unfashionable ☐
21. unemploymence ☐
22. whine ☐

SCORE ______ /22

TEST 30.9

1. absorebent ☐
2. bridegroom ☐
3. convert ☐
4. disatissfied ☐
5. dual ☐
6. emperor ☐
7. extracurricula ☐
8. forword ☐
9. guidence ☐
10. incouragement ☐
11. inaudible ☐
12. iritation ☐
13. lessen ☐
14. mouthes ☐
15. presidential ☐
16. suitte ☐
17. stewerd ☐
18. subdivision ☐
19. tolled ☐
20. torpedoes ☐
21. unbearable ☐
22. warlock ☐

SCORE ______ /22

TEST 30.10

1. actress ☐
2. axes ☐
3. bazaar ☐
4. bossess ☐
5. classifiable ☐
6. crescendos ☐
7. disturbancy ☐
8. forensically ☐
9. hoarde ☐
10. inelegible ☐
11. insignifficance ☐
12. ireplaceable ☐
13. laps ☐
14. mowed ☐
15. misremmembered ☐
16. persceptible ☐
17. rhinocerii ☐
18. succession ☐
19. trecked ☐
20. unremarkabley ☐
21. unpatriotical ☐
22. widow ☐

SCORE ______ /22

TEST 30.11

1. autonymous ☐
2. borders ☐
3. coherrence ☐
4. chiefs ☐
5. disrespectfull ☐
6. floging ☐
7. guerrilla ☐
8. hangers ☐
9. hysterically ☐
10. inprudence ☐
11. mosquitoe ☐
12. prologue ☐
13. quartz ☐
14. sultana ☐
15. their's ☐
16. transfering ☐
17. unacknowledged ☐
18. ungramatical ☐
19. unrepentent ☐
20. unresolveble ☐
21. waltszes ☐
22. wreek ☐

SCORE ______ /22

TEST 30.12

1. archipelagoes ☐
2. bachelour ☐
3. confectionerie ☐
4. conscientious ☐
5. differed ☐
6. disoreiented ☐
7. erossion ☐
8. extraterrestral ☐
9. fêtes's ☐
10. intervene ☐
11. irretrievable ☐
12. naval ☐
13. proficieancy ☐
14. rhetoritian ☐
15. shephardess ☐
16. subcontinent ☐
17. superscede ☐
18. transgression ☐
19. unabridged ☐
20. uncomprommising ☐
21. whet ☐
22. zeroes ☐

SCORE ______ /22

ANSWERS

Please note the following:
(1) As indicated at the beginning of this book, in most cases, there is only one correct answer to each question. In the few cases where there is more than one correct answer, all correct alternative spellings are provided.
(2) Obscure, archaic, and American spellings are not included.
(3) In the Revision Units (i.e. Units 6, 12, 18, 24, & 30) only one possible correct spelling for each misspelt word is listed.

UNIT 1

(1) tomorrow
(2) Forty
(3) criticises
(4) identity
(5) variety
(6) probably
(7) awkward
(8) occupied
(9) developing
(10) familiar
(11) relevant
(12) amateur
(13) harassed
(14) definite
(15) twelfth
(16) Wednesday
(17) attached
(18) category
(19) bruised
(20) wonderful

(21) - (30) *The 10 incorrectly spelt words and their correct spellings are as follows:*
occassion ⇨ occasion
parliment ⇨ parliament
dictionery ⇨ dictionary
explaination ⇨ explanation
embarass ⇨ embarrass
programe ⇨ programme
compitition ⇨ competition
corespond ⇨ correspond
nieghbour ⇨ neighbour
secretry ⇨ secretary

(31) ✗ ⇨ necessary

(32) ✗ ⇨ government
(33) ✗ ⇨ pronunciation
(34) ✗ ⇨ temperature
(35) ✓
(36) ✗ ⇨ vegetable
(37) ✓
(38) ✗ ⇨ restaurant
(39) ✓

(40) ✗ (⇨ disappear)
(41) ✗ (⇨ strength)
(42) ✓
(43) ✗ (⇨ medicine)
(44) ✗ (⇨ exercise)
(45) ✓
(46) ✓
(47) ✓
(48) ✗ (⇨ address)
(49) ✗ (⇨ calendar)
(50) ✗ (⇨ separate)
(51) ✗ (⇨ ordinary)
(52) ✓
(53) ✓
(54) ✗ (⇨ particular)
(55) ✗ (⇨ height)
(56) ✓
(57) ✓
(58) ✓
(59) ✗ (⇨ favourite)
(60) ✓
(61) ✓
(62) ✓
(63) ✗ (⇨ through OR thorough)
(64) ✓
(65) ✗ (⇨ surprise)
(66) ✓
(67) ✗ (⇨ remember)
(68) ✓
(69) ✓
(70) ✗ (⇨ decide)
(71) ✓
(72) ✗ (⇨ perhaps)
(73) ✓
(74) ✗ (⇨ century)
(75) ✗ (⇨ interest)
(76) ✓
(77) ✗ (⇨ therefore)
(78) ✗ (⇨ sentence)
(79) ✗ (⇨ grammar)
(80) ✓
(81) ✓

(82) controvesy (⇨ controversy)
(83) determinacion (⇨ determination)
(84) interupted (⇨ interrupted)
(85) reccomend (⇨ recommend)
(86) Curiousity (⇨ Curiosity)
(87) sacrafice (⇨ sacrifice)
(88) prejuidice (⇨ prejudice)
(89) Febuary (⇨ February)
(90) desprately (⇨ desperately)
(91) comittee (⇨ committee)
(92) accompniament (⇨ accompaniment)
(93) arguement (⇨ argument)
(94) Eight (⇨ Eighth)
(95) langages (⇨ languages)
(96) occurences (⇨ occurrences)
(97) comunication (⇨ communication)
(98) enviroment (⇨ environment)
(99) actuall (⇨ actual)
(100) sinscerity (⇨ sincerity)

(101) All 3 are correct
(102) shoulder
(103) knowledge
(104) complete
(105) continue
(106) All 3 are incorrect
(107) describe; frequently
(108) All 3 are incorrect
(109) expertise
(110) develop; soldier
(111) parallel
(112) material
(113) All 3 are correct
(114) All 3 are incorrect
(115) rhyme; thought

(116) B. woman ... breath
(117) C. questions ... difficult
(118) D. increase ... busy
(119) A. arrive ... early
(120) C. guide ... promised
(121) B. enough ... pressure
(122) D. notice ... opposite
(123) A. regular ... occasionally
(124) C. positions ... though

UNIT 2

(1) reincarnation
(2) coincide
(3) anti-inflammatory
(4) co-operation

(5) reimburse
(6) collaborate
(7) de-emphasise
(8) deduce
(9) antihero OR anti-hero
(10) re-employ
(11) recurring
(12) semicircle
(13) reduce
(14) collision
(15) redeem

(16) <u>re</u>-enter
(17) <u>co</u>-ordination
(18) <u>semi</u>-automatic OR <u>semi</u>automatic
(19) <u>re</u>designed
(20) <u>micro</u>biologist
(21) <u>de</u>-escalate
(22) <u>re</u>-editing
(23) <u>anti</u>bodies
(24) <u>co</u>-organisers
(25) <u>semi</u>colon
(26) <u>de</u>moted
(27) <u>re</u>-examining
(28) <u>anti</u>social
(29) <u>re</u>-elected
(30) <u>co</u>-operate
(31) <u>micro</u>-organism

(1) fr__nd ⇨ fr<u>ie</u>nd
(2) l__sure ⇨ l<u>ei</u>sure
(3) anx__ty ⇨ anx<u>ie</u>ty
(4) conven__nt ⇨ conven<u>ie</u>nt
(5) r__gn ⇨ r<u>ei</u>gn
(6) fr__ght ⇨ fr<u>ei</u>ght
(7) for__gn ⇨ for<u>ei</u>gn
(8) __derdown ⇨ <u>ei</u>derdown
(9) impat__nt ⇨ impat<u>ie</u>nt
(10) br__fcase ⇨ br<u>ie</u>fcase
(11) w__ght ⇨ w<u>ei</u>ght
(12) n__ghbourhood ⇨ n<u>ei</u>ghbourhood
(13) y__ld ⇨ y<u>ie</u>ld
(14) r__ndeer ⇨ r<u>ei</u>ndeer
(15) sover__gn ⇨ sover<u>ei</u>gn
(16) hyg__ne ⇨ hyg<u>ie</u>ne
(17) gondol__r ⇨ gondol<u>ie</u>r

(18) ✓
(19) ✗ (rel<u>ie</u>ved ⇨ rel<u>ie</u>ved)
(20) ✗ (s<u>ie</u>zed ⇨ s<u>ei</u>zed)

(21) ✗ (bes<u>ei</u>ged ⇨ bes<u>ie</u>ged)
(22) ✓
(23) ✓
(24) ✗ (unv<u>ie</u>ling ⇨ unv<u>ei</u>ling)
(25) ✗ (ingred<u>ei</u>nt ⇨ ingred<u>ie</u>nt)
(26) ✓
(27) ✗ (len<u>ei</u>nt ⇨ len<u>ie</u>nt)
(28) ✓
(29) ✗ (l<u>ei</u>utenant ⇨ l<u>ie</u>utenant)
(30) ✗ (chandel<u>ei</u>r ⇨ chandel<u>ie</u>r)
(31) ✓
(32) ✗ (n<u>ei</u>ce ⇨ n<u>ie</u>ce)
(33) ✓
(34) ✗ (well-rec<u>ie</u>ved ⇨ well-rec<u>ie</u>ved)
(35) ✗ (b<u>ie</u>ge ⇨ b<u>ei</u>ge)

(1) A. cautious ... tiptoed
(2) D. vicious ... defenceless
(3) B. sailor ... precious
(4) D. Nutritious ... unappetising
(5) A. boring ... repetitious
(6) C. nonsense ... fictitious
(7) B. ambitious ... monotonous
(8) C. spacious ... luxurious
(9) D. voracious ... atrocious

(10) curious
(11) All 3 are correct
(12) anxious; suspicious
(13) superstitious; hideous
(14) dangerous; perilous
(15) conscious
(16) All 3 are incorrect
(17) tremendous; jealous
(18) All 3 are correct
(19) tedious; joyous
(20) All 3 are correct
(21) venomous
(22) ridiculous
(23) All 3 are incorrect
(24) All 3 are incorrect

(1) A. essential
(2) C. confidential
(3) D. artificial
(4) A. officials
(5) B. provincial
(6) C. special
(7) C. residential

(8) A. glacial
(9) D. social
(10) B. infomercials

(11) s u p e r f i c i a l
(12) f i n a n c i a l
(13) p a r t i a l
(14) c o m m e r c i a l
(15) p o t e n t i a l
(16) s e q u e n t i a l
(17) r a c i a l
(18) p a l a t i a l
(19) c r u c i a l
(20) i n f l u e n t i a l
(21) e s p e c i a l
(22) m a r t i a l
(23) i m p a r t i a l
(24) f a c i a l
(25) u n o f f i c i a l
(26) b e n e f i c i a l
(27) j u d i c i a l
(28) s u b s t a n t i a l

TEST 6.1

(1) ✓	**(8)** ✗	**(15)** ✗
(2) ✗	**(9)** ✓	**(16)** ✗
(3) ✗	**(10)** ✓	**(17)** ✗
(4) ✓	**(11)** ✗	**(18)** ✓
(5) ✗	**(12)** ✓	**(19)** ✗
(6) ✗	**(13)** ✓	**(20)** ✓
(7) ✗	**(14)** ✓	

(2) awkw<u>a</u>rd; (3) barb<u>a</u>rous; (5) complet<u>e</u>; (6) <u>de</u>duce; (7) excell<u>e</u>nt; (8) gri<u>e</u>ved; (11) occa<u>s</u>ion; (15) sacrifice; (16) suspi<u>c</u>ious; (17) twel<u>f</u>th; (19) vari<u>e</u>ty

TEST 6.2

(1) ✗	**(8)** ✓	**(15)** ✗
(2) ✗	**(9)** ✓	**(16)** ✗
(3) ✓	**(10)** ✗	**(17)** ✗
(4) ✓	**(11)** ✓	**(18)** ✓
(5) ✗	**(12)** ✗	**(19)** ✗
(6) ✓	**(13)** ✓	**(20)** ✗
(7) ✗	**(14)** ✗	

(1) ac<u>c</u>ompany; *(2)* ave<u>r</u>age; *(5)* confiden<u>ti</u>al; *(7)* exer<u>c</u>ise; *(10)* ma<u>l</u>icious; *(12)* particu<u>l</u>ar; *(14)* relev<u>a</u>nt; *(15)* rede<u>e</u>m; *(16)* scien<u>ti</u>fic; *(17)* sur<u>p</u>rise; *(19)* tre<u>m</u>endous; *(20)* vig<u>o</u>rous

(1) ambi<u>ti</u>ous; *(2)* arg<u>u</u>ment; *(3)* bes<u>ie</u>ged; *(5)* conv<u>e</u>nience; *(6)* dis<u>a</u>ppear; *(7)* exist<u>e</u>nce; *(9)* haza<u>r</u>dous; *(10)* inf<u>a</u>mous; *(13)* ordin<u>a</u>ry; *(19)* sover<u>ei</u>gn; *(21)* unveil<u>i</u>ng; *(22)* well-rec<u>ei</u>ved

(5) counterf<u>ei</u>t; *(6)* desper<u>a</u>tely; *(8)* eigh<u>th</u>; *(9)* fo<u>r</u>wards; *(10)* hum<u>o</u>ngous; *(11)* inf<u>o</u>mercials; *(12)* lux<u>u</u>rious; *(13)* mounta<u>i</u>nous; *(14)* pe<u>c</u>uliar; *(18)* repeti<u>ti</u>ous; *(19)* sin<u>c</u>erely; *(20)* signa<u>t</u>ure; *(21)* tomo<u>rr</u>ow

TEST 6.3

(1) ✗	(8) ✗	(15) ✓
(2) ✓	(9) ✓	(16) ✗
(3) ✗	(10) ✗	(17) ✓
(4) ✓	(11) ✓	(18) ✗
(5) ✗	(12) ✓	(19) ✓
(6) ✗	(13) ✗	(20) ✗
(7) ✓	(14) ✓	

(1) adventu<u>r</u>ous; *(3)* bel<u>ie</u>ve; *(5)* cur<u>i</u>osity; *(6)* desp<u>e</u>rate; *(8)* Febr<u>ua</u>ry; *(10)* imp<u>a</u>tient; *(13)* n<u>ie</u>ce; *(16)* pre<u>c</u>ious; *(18)* red<u>e</u>signed; *(20)* w<u>ei</u>rd

TEST 6.4

(1) ✓	(9) ✓	(17) ✗
(2) ✓	(10) ✗	(18) ✓
(3) ✗	(11) ✓	(19) ✓
(4) ✓	(12) ✓	(20) ✓
(5) ✗	(13) ✗	(21) ✗
(6) ✓	(14) ✗	(22) ✗
(7) ✗	(15) ✓	
(8) ✗	(16) ✓	

(3) ben<u>e</u>ficial; *(5)* controve<u>r</u>sy; *(7)* espe<u>c</u>ial; *(8)* favou<u>r</u>ite; *(10)* ha<u>r</u>assed; *(13)* microbiol<u>o</u>gist; *(14)* nutri<u>ti</u>ous; *(17)* prosp<u>e</u>rous; *(21)* super<u>fic</u>ial; *(22)* ve<u>n</u>omous

TEST 6.5

(1) ✗	(9) ✗	(17) ✓
(2) ✗	(10) ✗	(18) ✓
(3) ✗	(11) ✓	(19) ✓
(4) ✓	(12) ✓	(20) ✓
(5) ✗	(13) ✗	(21) ✗
(6) ✗	(14) ✓	(22) ✗
(7) ✗	(15) ✓	
(8) ✓	(16) ✓	

TEST 6.6

(1) ✓	(9) ✗	(17) ✗
(2) ✗	(10) ✓	(18) ✓
(3) ✓	(11) ✓	(19) ✓
(4) ✗	(12) ✗	(20) ✓
(5) ✗	(13) ✗	(21) ✗
(6) ✗	(14) ✗	(22) ✓
(7) ✓	(15) ✓	
(8) ✗	(16) ✗	

(2) atro<u>c</u>ious; *(4)* co<u>i</u>ncide; *(8)* fin<u>a</u>ncial; *(9)* herbiv<u>o</u>rous; *(12)* l<u>ie</u>utenant; *(13)* min<u>u</u>te; *(14)* posse<u>ss</u>ion; *(16)* rh<u>y</u>thm; *(17)* re-enter; *(21)* supersti<u>ti</u>ous

TEST 6.7

(1) ✗	(9) ✗	(17) ✓
(2) ✗	(10) ✗	(18) ✓
(3) ✓	(11) ✓	(19) ✓
(4) ✗	(12) ✓	(20) ✓
(5) ✗	(13) ✓	(21) ✗
(6) ✗	(14) ✗	(22) ✗
(7) ✗	(15) ✓	
(8) ✓	(16) ✗	

(1) am<u>a</u>teur; *(2)* arti<u>fic</u>ial; *(4)* collabo<u>r</u>ate; *(5)* co-ordin<u>a</u>tion; *(6)* deli<u>c</u>ious; *(7)* extr<u>e</u>me; *(9)* ficti<u>ti</u>ous; *(10)* hid<u>e</u>ous; *(14)* micro-organism; *(16)* outrag<u>eo</u>us; *(21)* spe<u>c</u>ial; *(22)* unappeti<u>s</u>ing

TEST 6.8

(1) ✓	(9) ✗	(17) ✓
(2) ✓	(10) ✗	(18) ✗
(3) ✓	(11) ✗	(19) ✗
(4) ✓	(12) ✗	(20) ✗
(5) ✗	(13) ✗	(21) ✗

TEST 6.9

(1) ✗	(9) ✓	(17) ✗
(2) ✓	(10) ✗	(18) ✗
(3) ✗	(11) ✗	(19) ✗
(4) ✓	(12) ✗	(20) ✗
(5) ✗	(13) ✓	(21) ✓
(6) ✗	(14) ✓	(22) ✗
(7) ✗	(15) ✗	
(8) ✗	(16) ✓	

(1) anti<u>h</u>ero; *(3)* brig<u>a</u>dier; *(5)* cons<u>c</u>ious; *(6)* disas<u>t</u>rous; *(7)* equip<u>m</u>ent; *(8)* espe<u>c</u>ially; *(10)* govern<u>m</u>ent; *(11)* hyg<u>ie</u>ne; *(12)* ingred<u>ie</u>nt; *(15)* per<u>i</u>lous; *(17)* rh<u>y</u>me; *(18)* rest<u>au</u>rant; *(19)* re-exami<u>n</u>ing; *(20)* secr<u>e</u>tary; *(22)* thund<u>e</u>rous

TEST 6.10

(1) ✗	(9) ✗	(17) ✓
(2) ✗	(10) ✓	(18) ✗
(3) ✗	(11) ✓	(19) ✗
(4) ✗	(12) ✗	(20) ✓
(5) ✓	(13) ✓	(21) ✗
(6) ✓	(14) ✗	(22) ✗
(7) ✗	(15) ✗	
(8) ✗	(16) ✗	

(1) acci<u>d</u>entally; *(2)* agg<u>r</u>essive; *(3)* bru<u>ise</u>d; *(4)* commi<u>tt</u>ee; *(7)* determin<u>a</u>tion; *(8)* environ<u>m</u>ent; *(9)* expl<u>a</u>nation; *(12)* ne<u>c</u>essary; *(14)* program<u>m</u>e; *(15)* re<u>c</u>urring; *(16)* re<u>i</u>ndeer; *(18)* spa<u>c</u>ious; *(19)* substan<u>ti</u>al; *(21)* therefo<u>r</u>e; *(22)* We<u>d</u>nesday

TEST 6.11

(1) ✗	(9) ✓	(17) ✓
(2) ✓	(10) ✗	(18) ✗
(3) ✓	(11) ✓	(19) ✓
(4) ✓	(12) ✗	(20) ✗
(5) ✓	(13) ✗	(21) ✗
(6) ✗	(14) ✗	(22) ✗
(7) ✗	(15) ✗	
(8) ✗	(16) ✓	

(1) accompaniment; (6) demoted; (7) disobedient; (8) embarrass; (10) grammar; (12) occurrences; (13) parliament; (14) pretentious; (15) recommend; (18) semicolon; (20) sincerity; (21) temperature; (22) yield

TEST 6.12

(1) ✗	(9) ✓	(17) ✓
(2) ✓	(10) ✓	(18) ✗
(3) ✓	(11) ✗	(19) ✓
(4) ✗	(12) ✓	(20) ✓
(5) ✓	(13) ✗	(21) ✗
(6) ✗	(14) ✗	(22) ✓
(7) ✓	(15) ✗	
(8) ✓	(16) ✗	

(1) anti-inflammatory; (4) convenient; (6) decaffeinated; (11) guarantee; (13) neighbourhood; (14) occasionally; (15) poltergeist; (16) pronunciation; (18) rebellious; (21) treacherous

UNIT 7

(1) <u>dis</u> + courage ⇨ <u>discourage</u>
(2) <u>mis</u> + lead ⇨ <u>mislead</u>
(3) <u>ir</u> + relevant ⇨ <u>irrelevant</u>
(4) <u>mis</u> + behave ⇨ <u>misbehave</u>
(5) <u>dis</u> + possess ⇨ <u>dispossess</u>
(6) <u>mis</u> + print ⇨ <u>misprint</u>
(7) <u>mis</u> + address ⇨ <u>misaddress</u>
(8) <u>ir</u> + regular ⇨ <u>irregular</u>
(9) <u>dis</u> + obey ⇨ <u>disobey</u>
(10) <u>mis</u> + govern ⇨ <u>misgovern</u>
(11) <u>il</u> + legal ⇨ <u>illegal</u>
(12) <u>dis</u> + count ⇨ <u>discount</u> OR
<u>mis</u> + count ⇨ <u>miscount</u>
(13) <u>dis</u> + agree ⇨ <u>disagree</u>
(14) <u>mis</u> + guide ⇨ <u>misguide</u>
(15) <u>mis</u> + heard ⇨ <u>misheard</u>
(16) <u>dis</u> + appoint ⇨ <u>disappoint</u>
(17) <u>il</u> + legible ⇨ <u>illegible</u>
(18) <u>ir</u> + rational ⇨ <u>irrational</u>
(19) <u>dis</u> + allow ⇨ <u>disallow</u>
(20) <u>dis</u> + regard ⇨ <u>disregard</u> OR
<u>mis</u> + regard ⇨ <u>misregard</u>
(21) <u>dis</u> + pose ⇨ <u>dispose</u>
(22) <u>mis</u> + fit ⇨ <u>misfit</u>
(23) <u>mis</u> + shaped ⇨ <u>misshaped</u>
(24) <u>dis</u> + arm ⇨ <u>disarm</u>
(25) <u>dis</u> + able ⇨ <u>disable</u>
(26) <u>mis</u> + align ⇨ <u>misalign</u>
(27) <u>mis</u> + conduct ⇨ <u>misconduct</u>
(28) <u>dis</u> + card ⇨ <u>discard</u>
(29) <u>dis</u> + grace ⇨ <u>disgrace</u>
(30) <u>dis</u> + honest ⇨ <u>dishonest</u>
(31) <u>mis</u> + handle ⇨ <u>mishandle</u>
(32) <u>mis</u> + label ⇨ <u>mislabel</u>

(33) illiterate
(34) disapproval
(35) misspelled OR misspelt
(36) irresponsible
(37) disappearance
(38) misremember
(39) dissatisfied
(40) discontinuing
(41) mistreatment
(42) disadvantage
(43) disagreeable
(44) illogical
(45) mistrustful
(46) irresistible
(47) disappointment
(48) misapprehension
(49) misdeed
(50) irreversible
(51) mislaid
(52) disembarked
(53) discourteous
(54) misdirection
(55) disassemble
(56) discomfort
(57) misinformation
(58) disenchanted
(59) misconception
(60) dissimilarity
(61) misapplied
(62) disruption
(63) misspeak
(64) disorderly
(65) misjudged
(66) dismissal
(67) illegitimate
(68) disbelievingly

UNIT 8

(1) ✗ ⇨ conc<u>ei</u>ve
(2) ✗ ⇨ mischi<u>e</u>vous
(3) ✓
(4) ✓
(5) ✗ ⇨ c<u>ei</u>ling
(6) ✓
(7) ✓
(8) ✓
(9) ✗ ⇨ ju<u>i</u>ciest
(10) ✗ ⇨ conci<u>e</u>rge
(11) ✓
(12) ✗ ⇨ r<u>e</u>ceipts
(13) ✓
(14) ✗ ⇨ financi<u>er</u>
(15) ✗ ⇨ p<u>ie</u>rcingly
(16) ✓
(17) ✗ ⇨ recip<u>es</u>
(18) ✓
(19) ✓
(20) ✗ ⇨ transc<u>ei</u>vers
(21) ✗ ⇨ conc<u>ei</u>tedness
(22) ✓

UNIT 9

(1) charity
(2) psyche
(3) crescent
(4) cyanide
(5) enchilada
(6) rye
(7) martyr
(8) crescendo
(9) archipelago
(10) gyroscope
(11) fluorescent

(12) ✗ (⇨ asym<u>m</u>etrical)
(13) ✓
(14) ✗ (⇨ sch<u>e</u>mes)
(15) ✗ (⇨ isos<u>c</u>eles)
(16) ✓
(17) ✓
(18) ✗ (⇨ <u>e</u>choing)
(19) ✗ (⇨ <u>C</u>hrysanthemums)
(20) ✗ (⇨ scen<u>e</u>ry)

(21) ✗ (⇨ plat<u>y</u>pus)
(22) ✓
(23) ✗ (⇨ archi<u>tec</u>t)
(24) ✗ (⇨ sus<u>c</u>eptible)
(25) ✗ (⇨ scep<u>tre</u>)
(26) ✓
(27) ✓
(28) ✓
(29) ✗ (⇨ s<u>c</u>holar)
(30) ✗ (⇨ hi<u>e</u>rarchical)

(31) <u>c</u>hef
(32) <u>t</u>ongue
(33) <u>m</u>oustache
(34) uni<u>q</u>ue
(35) m<u>achine</u>
(36) <u>L</u>eague
(37) brochure
(38) para<u>c</u>hute
(39) <u>c</u>halet
(40) an<u>ti</u>que
(41) <u>c</u>olleague<u>s</u>
(42) bou<u>ti</u>que
(43) pla<u>g</u>ue
(44) <u>c</u>hivalry
(45) bou<u>q</u>uet
(46) <u>c</u>handelier
(47) <u>c</u>atalogue
(48) <u>p</u>istachio
(49) <u>c</u>heque

(50) picturesque
(51) champagne
(52) racquet
(53) physique
(54) fuchsia
(55) grotesque
(56) arachnid
(57) question
(58) archive
(59) chasm
(60) opaque

(1) democratic + <u>ally</u> ⇨
<u>democratically</u>
(2) separate + <u>ly</u> ⇨ <u>separately</u>
(3) harsh + <u>ly</u> ⇨ <u>harshly</u>
(4) grave + <u>ly</u> ⇨ <u>gravely</u>
(5) Begrudging + <u>ly</u> ⇨
<u>Begrudgingly</u>
(6) literal + <u>ly</u> ⇨ <u>literally</u>
(7) flimsy + <u>ly</u> ⇨ <u>flimsily</u>

(8) magic + <u>ally</u> ⇨ <u>magically</u>
(9) naive + <u>ly</u> ⇨ <u>naively</u>
(10) persuasive + <u>ly</u> ⇨
<u>persuasively</u>
(11) complete + <u>ly</u> ⇨ <u>completely</u>
(12) abominable + <u>ly</u> ⇨
<u>abominably</u>
(13) ready + <u>ly</u> ⇨ <u>readily</u>
(14) Historic + <u>ally</u> ⇨ <u>Historically</u>
(15) Ordinary + <u>ly</u> ⇨ <u>Ordinarily</u>
(16) precise + <u>ly</u> ⇨ <u>precisely</u>
(17) cryptic + <u>ally</u> ⇨ <u>cryptically</u>
(18) hoarse + <u>ly</u> ⇨ <u>hoarsely</u>
(19) environment + <u>ally</u> ⇨
<u>environmentally</u>

(20) D. miserably
(21) B. basically
(22) C. immediately
(23) A. cheerily
(24) C. inexplicably
(25) D. pompously
(26) B. academically
(27) D. temporarily
(28) A. tangibly
(29) C. elaborately

(1) prevent + <u>able</u> ⇨ <u>preventable</u>
(2) envy + <u>able</u> ⇨ <u>enviable</u>
(3) apply + <u>able</u> ⇨ <u>applicable</u>
(4) mention + <u>able</u> ⇨
<u>mentionable</u>
(5) adore + <u>able</u> ⇨ <u>adorable</u>
(6) question + <u>able</u> ⇨
<u>questionable</u>
(7) admit + <u>ible</u> ⇨ <u>admissible</u>
(8) reverse + <u>ible</u> ⇨ <u>reversible</u>
(9) like + <u>able</u> ⇨ <u>likeable</u>
(10) answer + <u>able</u> ⇨
<u>answerable</u>
(11) construct + <u>able</u> OR <u>ible</u> ⇨
<u>constructable</u> OR <u>constructible</u>
(12) imagine + <u>able</u> ⇨
<u>imaginable</u>
(13) deny + <u>able</u> ⇨ <u>deniable</u>
(14) attach + <u>able</u> ⇨ <u>attachable</u>
(15) deduce + <u>ible</u> ⇨ <u>deducible</u>
(16) regret + <u>able</u> ⇨ <u>regrettable</u>
(17) knowledge + <u>able</u> ⇨
<u>knowledgeable</u>
(18) recommend + <u>able</u> ⇨
<u>recommendable</u>

(19) programme + <u>able</u> ⇨
<u>programmable</u>
(20) achieve + <u>able</u> ⇨ <u>achievable</u>
(21) vary + <u>able</u> ⇨ <u>variable</u>
(22) access + <u>ible</u> ⇨ <u>accessible</u>
(23) breathe + <u>able</u> ⇨
<u>breathable</u>
(24) suggest + <u>ible</u> ⇨ <u>suggestible</u>
(25) collapse + <u>ible</u> ⇨ <u>collapsible</u>
(26) destruct + <u>ible</u> ⇨
<u>destructible</u>
(27) tolerate + <u>able</u> ⇨ <u>tolerable</u>
(28) suppose + <u>able</u> ⇨
<u>supposable</u>
(29) divide + <u>ible</u> ⇨ <u>divisible</u>
(30) consume + <u>able</u> ⇨
<u>consumable</u>
(31) collect + <u>ible</u> ⇨ <u>collectible</u>
(32) appreciate + <u>able</u> ⇨
<u>appreciable</u>

(33) C. conclusion ... debatable
(34) B. damage ... considerably
(35) D. suggestion ... sensibly
(36) A. comfortable ... purchase
(37) D. legible ... impossible
(38) B. reliable ... changeable
(39) C. forcible ... persuadable
(40) C. dependably ... enjoyable
(41) A. noticeably ...
understandable

TEST 12.1

(1) ✗	**(8)** ✓	**(15)** ✓
(2) ✓	**(9)** ✗	**(16)** ✓
(3) ✓	**(10)** ✓	**(17)** ✓
(4) ✓	**(11)** ✓	**(18)** ✓
(5) ✓	**(12)** ✗	**(19)** ✓
(6) ✗	**(13)** ✗	**(20)** ✓
(7) ✗	**(14)** ✗	

*(1) achi<u>e</u>vable; (6) colleagues;
(7) di<u>s</u>able; (9) elaborately; (12)
immediately; (13) juic<u>i</u>est (14)
lite<u>r</u>al*

TEST 12.2

(1) ✗	(8) ✗	(15) ✗
(2) ✓	(9) ✓	(16) ✓
(3) ✗	(10) ✓	(17) ✓
(4) ✓	(11) ✓	(18) ✗
(5) ✓	(12) ✓	(19) ✗
(6) ✗	(13) ✗	(20) ✗
(7) ✗	(14) ✓	

(1) acce*ss*ible; *(3)* ban*q*uet; *(6)* champ*ag*ne; *(7)* disa*g*ree; *(8)* discoura*g*e; *(13)* i*ll*ogical; *(15)* mischie*v*ous; *(18)* per*s*uasive; *(19)* ra*cq*uet; *(20)* scept*re*

TEST 12.3

(1) ✗	(8) ✗	(15) ✗
(2) ✗	(9) ✓	(16) ✗
(3) ✗	(10) ✗	(17) ✓
(4) ✗	(11) ✓	(18) ✗
(5) ✗	(12) ✗	(19) ✗
(6) ✓	(13) ✗	(20) ✓
(7) ✓	(14) ✗	

(1) ab*o*minable; *(2)* begrud*g*ing; *(3)* conc*ei*ve; *(4)* collectible; *(5)* chand*e*lier; *(8)* di*s*appoint; *(10)* fi*n*ancier; *(12)* i*rr*ational; *(13)* lea*g*ue; *(14)* mi*s*fit; *(15)* mis*s*pelt; *(16)* miser*a*bly; *(18)* piercin*g*ly; *(19)* para*c*hute

TEST 12.4

(1) ✓	(9) ✓	(17) ✗
(2) ✗	(10) ✗	(18) ✓
(3) ✓	(11) ✓	(19) ✗
(4) ✓	(12) ✓	(20) ✗
(5) ✗	(13) ✓	(21) ✗
(6) ✗	(14) ✗	(22) ✓
(7) ✗	(15) ✗	
(8) ✗	(16) ✓	

(2) avalanch*e*; *(5)* chor*u*s; *(6)* charact*er*; *(7)* dec*ei*vers; *(8)* di*s*appearance; *(10)* enjoy*a*ble; *(14)* mi*s*applied; *(15)* mention*a*ble; *(17)* pla*gu*e;

(19) sch*e*me; *(20)* squel*ch*; *(21)* tol*e*rable

TEST 12.5

(1) ✗	(9) ✓	(17) ✓
(2) ✓	(10) ✗	(18) ✗
(3) ✗	(11) ✗	(19) ✗
(4) ✓	(12) ✓	(20) ✓
(5) ✓	(13) ✗	(21) ✓
(6) ✗	(14) ✗	(22) ✗
(7) ✗	(15) ✗	
(8) ✓	(16) ✓	

(1) admi*ss*ible; *(3)* consu*m*able; *(6)* dedu*c*ible; *(7)* di*s*approval; *(10)* gym*n*asium; *(11)* inexpli*c*ably; *(13)* misinfo*r*mation; *(14)* misl*ai*d; *(15)* mis*s*peak; *(18)* regre*tt*able; *(19)* societi*e*s; *(22)* scen*er*y

TEST 12.6

(1) ✗	(9) ✓	(17) ✓
(2) ✗	(10) ✓	(18) ✗
(3) ✗	(11) ✓	(19) ✗
(4) ✗	(12) ✗	(20) ✓
(5) ✓	(13) ✓	(21) ✗
(6) ✗	(14) ✓	(22) ✗
(7) ✗	(15) ✓	
(8) ✓	(16) ✓	

(1) ador*a*ble; *(2)* appr*e*ciate; *(3)* crypti*c*; *(4)* comfort*a*ble; *(6)* dem*o*cratic; *(7)* di*s*assemble; *(12)* i*ll*iterate; *(18)* read*i*ly; *(19)* sep*a*rate; *(21)* syno*n*ym; *(22)* transc*ei*vers

TEST 12.7

(1) ✓	(9) ✓	(17) ✗
(2) ✗	(10) ✓	(18) ✓
(3) ✗	(11) ✗	(19) ✓
(4) ✗	(12) ✓	(20) ✗
(5) ✗	(13) ✓	(21) ✓
(6) ✗	(14) ✗	(22) ✗
(7) ✗	(15) ✗	
(8) ✓	(16) ✓	

(2) a*q*ueduct; *(3)* collap*s*ible; *(4)* cons*c*ience; *(5)* chape*r*one; *(6)* deni*a*ble; *(7)* di*s*missal; *(11)* i*rr*esponsible; *(14)* moust*ache*; *(15)* mis*s*haped; *(17)* persuad*a*ble; *(20)* suppos*a*ble; *(22)* tangi*b*ly

TEST 12.8

(1) ✗	(9) ✓	(17) ✗
(2) ✓	(10) ✗	(18) ✓
(3) ✗	(11) ✗	(19) ✗
(4) ✓	(12) ✓	(20) ✓
(5) ✗	(13) ✓	(21) ✗
(6) ✗	(14) ✓	(22) ✓
(7) ✓	(15) ✗	
(8) ✓	(16) ✓	

(1) appli*c*able; *(3)* conc*ie*rge; *(5)* charismati*c*; *(6)* destructible; *(10)* irr*e*levant; *(11)* knowled*ge*able; *(15)* prevent*a*ble; *(17)* recommend*a*ble; *(19)* techni*q*ue; *(21)* temp*o*rarily

TEST 12.9

(1) ✗	(9) ✗	(17) ✓
(2) ✓	(10) ✗	(18) ✗
(3) ✓	(11) ✗	(19) ✗
(4) ✓	(12) ✗	(20) ✗
(5) ✗	(13) ✗	(21) ✗
(6) ✗	(14) ✓	(22) ✓
(7) ✗	(15) ✗	
(8) ✓	(16) ✓	

(1) appreci*a*ble; *(5)* che*q*ue; *(6)* cha*uff*eur; *(7)* di*s*appointment; *(9)* divi*s*ible; *(10)* fl*uo*rescent; *(11)* gyr*o*scope; *(12)* irr*e*sistible; *(13)* i*ll*egal; *(15)* mistrustf*ul*; *(18)* pla*qu*e; *(19)* sensi*b*ly; *(20)* tympani; *(21)* unperc*ei*ved

TEST 12.10

(1) ✓	(9) ✓	(17) ✓
(2) ✓	(10) ✗	(18) ✓
(3) ✓	(11) ✓	(19) ✗
(4) ✓	(12) ✓	(20) ✗

(5) ×   (13) ×   (21) ×
(6) ✓   (14) ×   (22) ✓
(7) ×   (15) ✓
(8) ×   (16) ✓

(5) considerably; (7) damage; (8) deficiency; (10) dispossess; (13) historically; (14) irreversible; (19) programmable; (20) psyche; (21) recipes

TEST 12.11

(1) ✓   (9) ✓   (17) ×
(2) ×   (10) ×   (18) ✓
(3) ×   (11) ×   (19) ×
(4) ✓   (12) ✓   (20) ×
(5) ✓   (13) ×   (21) ×
(6) ×   (14) ×   (22) ×
(7) ✓   (15) ✓
(8) ×   (16) ✓

(2) bronchitis; (3) catalogue; (6) debatable; (8) discontinuing; (10) dissatisfied; (11) equestrian; (13) hoarsely; (14) illegitimate; (17) pistachio; (19) queasy; (20) reversible; (21) syndicate; (22) suggestible

TEST 12.12

(1) ×   (9) ✓   (17) ×
(2) ✓   (10) ×   (18) ×
(3) ×   (11) ×   (19) ×
(4) ×   (12) ×   (20) ×
(5) ×   (13) ×   (21) ×
(6) ×   (14) ✓   (22) ✓
(7) ×   (15) ✓
(8) ×   (16) ×

(1) abominably; (3) chrysanthemums; (4) conceitedness; (5) crèche; (6) dependably; (7) disadvantage; (8) disagreeable; (10) disembarked; (11) dissimilarity; (12) effervescent; (13) gymkhana; (16) illegible; (17) martyr; (18) misapprehension;

(19) naively; (20) omniscient; (21) photosynthesis

(1) immature
(2) inattentive
(3) incorrect
(4) imbalance
(5) inadvisable
(6) immortal
(7) impatient
(8) indefinite
(9) imprudent
(10) infamous
(11) inadequate
(12) impractical
(13) insufficient
(14) imprecise
(15) injustice
(16) invalid
(17) immoral
(18) inedible
(19) immoveable

(20) review
(21) immigrate
(22) indirect
(23) renovate
(24) implied
(25) intake
(26) rejected
(27) replay
(28) refused
(29) intersects
(30) informed
(31) imported
(32) reconnect
(33) repelled
(34) inactive
(35) intermediate
(36) incur
(37) impaired
(38) inclined

(39) inter + national ⇨ international
(40) re + decorate ⇨ redecorate
(41) im + prove ⇨ improve
(42) in + humane ⇨ inhumane
(43) in + accurate ⇨ inaccurate
(44) re + act ⇨ react OR inter + act ⇨ interact
(45) re + claim ⇨ reclaim
(46) inter + change ⇨ interchange
(47) im + polite ⇨ impolite
(48) re + acquaint ⇨ reacquaint
(49) in + formal ⇨ informal
(50) inter + city ⇨ intercity
(51) im + plant ⇨ implant OR re + plant ⇨ replant
(52) inter + library ⇨ interlibrary
(53) re + fund ⇨ refund
(54) re + consider ⇨ reconsider
(55) in + destructible ⇨ indestructible
(56) im + personal ⇨ impersonal OR inter + personal ⇨ interpersonal
(57) re + mission ⇨ remission OR inter + mission ⇨ intermission
(58) in + capable ⇨ incapable
(59) in + dignity ⇨ indignity
(60) re + boot ⇨ reboot
(61) im + mobile ⇨ immobile
(62) in + compatible ⇨ incompatible
(63) inter + twine ⇨ intertwine
(64) re + generate ⇨ regenerate
(65) in + separable ⇨ inseparable
(66) im + plausible ⇨ implausible
(67) im + material ⇨ immaterial
(68) inter + galactic ⇨ intergalactic
(69) in + conclusive ⇨ inconclusive
(70) im + pertinent ⇨ impertinent

(1) cough
(2) route
(3) vow
(4) trout
(5) cower
(6) trough
(7) rogue
(8) draught
(9) borough
(10) chart
(11) south
(12) pout
(13) throat
(14) allow

(15) bout
(16) hiccough

UNIT 15

(1) doubts; b
(2) muscle; c
(3) island; s
(4) biscuits; u
(5) lamb; b
(6) vehicles; h
(7) business; i
(8) solemnly; n
(9) succumbed; b
(10) thistle; t
(11) cologne; g

(12) fascinated
(13) archaeologist
(14) nuisance
(15) queued
(16) wrinkled
(17) scent
(18) wreck
(19) rhymes
(20) receipt
(21) rustling
(22) chemicals
(23) guarantees
(24) gnashed
(25) pneumonia
(26) disguise
(27) debt
(28) knapsack
(29) campaigning
(30) Catacombs

UNIT 16

(1) observe ⇨ observant; observance
(2) differ ⇨ different; difference
(3) hinder ⇨ hindrance
(4) obey ⇨ obedient; obedience
(5) hesitate ⇨ hesitant; hesitancy OR hesitance
(6) expect ⇨ expectant; expectancy OR expectance
(7) reside ⇨ resident; residence; residency
(8) assist ⇨ assistant; assistance
(9) correspond ⇨ correspondent; correspondence
(10) suffice ⇨ sufficient; sufficiency
(11) survey ⇨ surveillance
(12) depend ⇨ dependant; dependent; dependence; dependency

(13) increment (incremence ✗)
(14) substance (substence ✗)
(15) tolerance (tolerence ✗)
(16) independent (independant ✗)
(17) insistent (insistant ✗)
(18) disobedience (disobedeience ✗)
(19) negligent (negligient ✗)
(20) recipient (recipiant ✗)
(21) resilience (resiliance ✗)
(22) component (componant ✗)
(23) lenience (leniance ✗)
(24) incompetence (incompetency ✗)

UNIT 17

(1) alter
(2) draft
(3) Practice
(4) guessed
(5) mourning
(6) Steel
(7) who's
(8) brews
(9) hart
(10) accept
(11) principal
(12) stationery
(13) led
(14) bawl
(15) Great
(16) wary
(17) devise
(18) serial
(19) assent
(20) further
(21) bridal
(22) profit
(23) effect
(24) herd
(25) dessert
(26) complements
(27) aisle
(28) proceed
(29) lightening
(30) meddle

(31) licence
(32) past
(33) aloud
(34) dissent
(35) prophesy
(36) missed
(37) whether
(38) advice
(39) current
(40) patience
(41) wrung

UNIT 18

TEST 18.1

(1) ✓	**(8)** ✓	**(15)** ✓
(2) ✗	**(9)** ✗	**(16)** ✓
(3) ✓	**(10)** ✗	**(17)** ✗
(4) ✓	**(11)** ✓	**(18)** ✓
(5) ✗	**(12)** ✓	**(19)** ✗
(6) ✓	**(13)** ✗	**(20)** ✓
(7) ✗	**(14)** ✓	

(2) bout; **(5)** different; **(7)** except; **(9)** immaterial; **(10)** impatient; **(13)** inefficiency; **(17)** obedient; **(19)** residency

TEST 18.2

(1) ✗	**(8)** ✗	**(15)** ✓
(2) ✓	**(9)** ✓	**(16)** ✗
(3) ✗	**(10)** ✗	**(17)** ✗
(4) ✗	**(11)** ✗	**(18)** ✗
(5) ✗	**(12)** ✗	**(19)** ✓
(6) ✗	**(13)** ✓	**(20)** ✗
(7) ✓	**(14)** ✗	

(1) assistance; **(3)** cereal; **(4)** chemicals; **(5)** dependence; **(6)** disguise; **(8)** hesitant; **(10)** impersonal; **(11)** incapable; **(12)** informal; **(14)** intersects; **(16)** mourning; **(17)** nought; **(18)** pout; **(20)** serial

TEST 18.3

(1) ✗	**(8)** ✗	**(15)** ✗
(2) ✓	**(9)** ✓	**(16)** ✗

(3) ✓	(10) ✓	(17) ✗
(4) ✓	(11) ✗	(18) ✗
(5) ✗	(12) ✗	(19) ✓
(6) ✓	(13) ✓	(20) ✗
(7) ✗	(14) ✓	

(1) a*ss*ent; *(5)* de*c*ency; *(7)* fough*t*; *(8)* imm*i*grate; *(11)* indefin*i*te; *(12)* inhum*a*ne; *(15)* inval*i*d; *(16)* l*e*nience; *(17)* mus*cl*e; *(18)* princip*l*e; *(20)* station*e*ry

TEST 18.4

(1) ✓	(9) ✗	(17) ✓
(2) ✓	(10) ✗	(18) ✗
(3) ✗	(11) ✓	(19) ✓
(4) ✗	(12) ✓	(20) ✓
(5) ✗	(13) ✓	(21) ✓
(6) ✓	(14) ✓	(22) ✗
(7) ✓	(15) ✗	
(8) ✓	(16) ✗	

(3) compet*e*nce; *(4)* di*ss*ent; *(5)* differ*e*nce; *(9)* imp*o*lite; *(10)* ined*i*ble; *(15)* nui*s*ance; *(16)* proceed; *(18)* rea*c*quaint; *(22)* th*o*rough

TEST 18.5

(1) ✗	(9) ✗	(17) ✓
(2) ✓	(10) ✓	(18) ✓
(3) ✗	(11) ✓	(19) ✓
(4) ✗	(12) ✗	(20) ✓
(5) ✓	(13) ✗	(21) ✗
(6) ✗	(14) ✓	(22) ✗
(7) ✗	(15) ✓	
(8) ✓	(16) ✓	

(1) appa*r*ent; *(3)* co*l*ogne; *(4)* caugh*t*; *(6)* fa*sc*inated; *(7)* hind*r*ance; *(9)* impractical; *(12)* li*c*ence; *(13)* med*dl*e; *(21)* w*h*ether; *(22)* wrin*k*led

TEST 18.6

| (1) ✓ | (9) ✗ | (17) ✓ |
| (2) ✓ | (10) ✓ | (18) ✓ |

(3) ✗	(11) ✗	(19) ✓
(4) ✓	(12) ✗	(20) ✓
(5) ✗	(13) ✓	(21) ✗
(6) ✓	(14) ✓	(22) ✗
(7) ✗	(15) ✗	
(8) ✓	(16) ✓	

(3) cur*r*ant; *(5)* de*bt*; *(7)* hic*c*ough; *(9)* imm*o*bile; *(11)* inseparable; *(12)* interlib*r*ary; *(15)* persist*e*nt; *(21)* solem*n*ly; *(22)* *w*rought

TEST 18.7

(1) ✗	(9) ✗	(17) ✓
(2) ✓	(10) ✗	(18) ✗
(3) ✗	(11) ✗	(19) ✗
(4) ✗	(12) ✓	(20) ✗
(5) ✗	(13) ✓	(21) ✓
(6) ✓	(14) ✓	(22) ✓
(7) ✗	(15) ✓	
(8) ✓	(16) ✗	

(1) assist*a*nt; *(3)* compl*e*ments; *(4)* coug*h*; *(5)* depend*e*ncy; *(7)* impai*r*ed; *(9)* ina*cc*urate; *(10)* increment; *(11)* observ*a*nce; *(16)* rh*y*mes; *(18)* *s*ought; *(19)* this*t*le; *(20)* thought

TEST 18.8

(1) ✗	(9) ✗	(17) ✗
(2) ✓	(10) ✓	(18) ✓
(3) ✓	(11) ✓	(19) ✓
(4) ✗	(12) ✗	(20) ✓
(5) ✗	(13) ✓	(21) ✗
(6) ✗	(14) ✓	(22) ✗
(7) ✓	(15) ✗	
(8) ✓	(16) ✗	

(1) a*l*tar; *(4)* defiant; *(5)* enduran*c*e; *(6)* f*r*aught; *(9)* insuffi*c*ient; *(12)* negli*g*ent; *(15)* re*c*eipt; *(16)* rust*l*ing; *(17)* substan*c*e; *(21)* wre*c*k; *(22)* vehi*cl*es

TEST 18.9

(1) ✓	(9) ✓	(17) ✓
(2) ✓	(10) ✗	(18) ✗
(3) ✗	(11) ✓	(19) ✓
(4) ✓	(12) ✓	(20) ✗
(5) ✗	(13) ✓	(21) ✗
(6) ✓	(14) ✗	(22) ✓
(7) ✓	(15) ✓	
(8) ✓	(16) ✓	

(3) correspond*e*nt; *(5)* fu*r*ther; *(10)* malevol*e*nt; *(14)* re*g*enerate; *(18)* thro*at*; *(20)* toler*a*nce; *(21)* *w*eather

TEST 18.10

(1) ✓	(9) ✓	(17) ✗
(2) ✗	(10) ✓	(18) ✗
(3) ✓	(11) ✓	(19) ✓
(4) ✗	(12) ✓	(20) ✓
(5) ✗	(13) ✗	(21) ✗
(6) ✗	(14) ✗	(22) ✗
(7) ✓	(15) ✓	
(8) ✗	(16) ✓	

(2) arch*ae*ologist; *(4)* compl*i*ment; *(5)* coher*e*nt; *(6)* des*c*ent; *(8)* efficien*y*; *(13)* imp*e*rtinent; *(14)* inad*e*quate; *(17)* li*c*ense; *(18)* prin*c*iple; *(21)* suffici*e*ncy; *(22)* throug*h*out

TEST 18.11

(1) ✗	(9) ✓	(17) ✗
(2) ✗	(10) ✗	(18) ✗
(3) ✓	(11) ✗	(19) ✓
(4) ✓	(12) ✓	(20) ✗
(5) ✗	(13) ✓	(21) ✗
(6) ✓	(14) ✓	(22) ✓
(7) ✓	(15) ✗	
(8) ✗	(16) ✗	

(1) a*l*oud; *(2)* brid*al*; *(5)* catac*o*mbs; *(8)* expect*a*nt; *(10)* immov*a*ble; *(11)* impre*c*ise; *(15)* med*dl*e; *(16)* observ*a*nt; *(17)* prec*e*de; *(18)* proph*et*; *(20)* recu*r*;

(21) surveill*a*nce

TEST 18.12

(1) ✗	**(9)** ✗	**(17)** ✗
(2) ✗	**(10)** ✗	**(18)** ✗
(3) ✗	**(11)** ✗	**(19)** ✗
(4) ✗	**(12)** ✓	**(20)** ✓
(5) ✓	**(13)** ✓	**(21)** ✗
(6) ✗	**(14)** ✗	**(22)** ✓
(7) ✗	**(15)** ✗	
(8) ✓	**(16)** ✓	

(1) assu*r*ances; *(2)* b*o*rough; *(3)* correspond*e*nce; *(4)* campai*gn*ing; *(6)* eloquen*c*e; *(7)* fu*r*lough; *(9)* implaus*i*ble; *(10)* imprudent; *(11)* indestruc*ti*ble; *(14)* *k*napsack; *(15)* lighte*n*ing; *(17)* pne*u*monia; *(18)* resil*i*ence; *(19)* recip*ie*nt; *(21)* su*c*cumbed

(1) super (*super*market)
(2) sub (*sub*committee)
(3) anti (*anti*septic)
(4) sub (*sub*categories)
(5) super (*super*stars)
(6) auto (*auto*graph)
(7) sub (*sub*conscious)
(8) anti (*anti*climax)
(9) sub (*sub*marine)
(10) auto (*auto*biographies)

(11) *anti*clockwise
(12) *super*natural
(13) *sub*title
(14) *super*human
(15) *sub*tract
(16) *anti*-theft OR *anti*theft
(17) *super*man
(18) *sub*merged
(19) *auto*mobiles
(20) *super*glue
(21) *anti*biotic
(22) *super*imposed
(23) *sub*divided
(24) *Sub*way
(25) *sub*heading
(26) *super*computers
(27) *sub*editor

(1) girls
(2) knaves
(3) tomatoes
(4) celebrations
(5) women
(6) mice
(7) ibises
(8) anniversaries
(9) feet
(10) men
(11) sheep
(12) privileges
(13) rhythms
(14) oxen
(15) igloos
(16) children
(17) teeth
(18) geese
(19) distilleries
(20) attendees
(21) foxes
(22) these
(23) miniatures
(24) wives
(25) cacti OR cactuses
(26) liabilities
(27) lice
(28) volcanoes OR volcanos
(29) allegories
(30) loaves
(31) crises
(32) deer
(33) those
(34) phenomena

(35) children's
(36) soldiers'
(37) fishes
(38) glasses
(39) shoes'
(40) controversies
(41) scarves
(42) amateurs'
(43) firemen's
(44) cookies
(45) radios'
(46) People's
(47) Cliffs
(48) fungi
(49) avocados
(50) quizzes'
(51) oases
(52) puppies'
(53) series
(54) hippopotamuses

(1) beginner
(2) gardener
(3) communicator
(4) forgotten
(5) limitation
(6) equipped
(7) sunburnt OR sunburned
(8) shipping
(9) occurring
(10) nagging
(11) preparations
(12) acquitted
(13) engineer
(14) bargaining
(15) overpopulation
(16) babysitter
(17) shouldered
(18) strummed
(19) carrier

(20) C. CCOMMODATE ⇨ a*c*commodated
(21) A. NSURIN ⇨ *i*nsuring
(22) D. ORMATTE ⇨ *f*ormatted
(23) C. MITTIN ⇨ e*mitti*ng
(24) B. NFOCUSE ⇨ *un*focuse*d*
(25) D. MBARRASSMEN ⇨ *e*mbarrassmen*t*
(26) B. EVELOPMEN ⇨ *d*evelopmen*t*
(27) D. AVESDROPPE ⇨ *e*avesdroppe*r*
(28) A. RONOUNCE ⇨ *p*ronounce*d*
(29) C. XAGGERATE ⇨ e*x*aggerate*d*

(1) deferral ✓
confe*rr*ence ✗ ⇨ confe*r*ence
diff*r*ence ✗ ⇨ diff*er*ence
suffe*rr*ed ✗ ⇨ suffe*r*ed
(2) offered ✓
infe*r*ed ✗ ⇨ infe*rr*ed
su*rf*fing ✗ ⇨ su*rfi*ng
refe*r*ance ✗ ⇨ refe*r*ence
(3) preference ✓

refe<u>r</u>al ✗ ⇨ refe<u>rr</u>al
diffe<u>rr</u>ing ✗ ⇨ diffe<u>r</u>ing
confe<u>r</u>ed ✗ ⇨ confe<u>rr</u>ed
(4) refereed ✓
refe<u>rr</u>endum ✗ ⇨ refe<u>r</u>endum
transfe<u>r</u>ance ✗ ⇨ transfe<u>r</u>ance
pilfe<u>rr</u>ing ✗ ⇨ pilfe<u>r</u>ing

(5) B. deference
(6) A. conferring
(7) C. deferred
(8) D. offering
(9) A. inference
(10) B. pilfered
(11) C. suffering
(12) A. surfer
(13) D. preferred
(14) B. interfere

UNIT 23

(1) music + <u>cian</u> ⇨ <u>musician</u>
(2) commit + <u>ssion</u> ⇨
commi<u>ssion</u>
(3) decide + <u>sion</u> ⇨ deci<u>sion</u>
(4) educate + <u>tion</u> ⇨ educa<u>tion</u>
(5) discuss + <u>ssion</u> ⇨ discu<u>ssion</u>
(6) adopt + <u>tion</u> ⇨ adop<u>tion</u>
(7) include + <u>sion</u> ⇨ inclu<u>sion</u>
(8) operate + <u>tion</u> ⇨ opera<u>tion</u>
(9) suggest + <u>tion</u> ⇨ sugges<u>tion</u>
(10) electric + <u>cian</u> ⇨ electri<u>cian</u>
(11) predict + <u>tion</u> ⇨ predic<u>tion</u>
(12) express + <u>ssion</u> ⇨
expre<u>ssion</u>
(13) submit + <u>ssion</u> ⇨
submi<u>ssion</u>
(14) elect + <u>tion</u> ⇨ elec<u>tion</u>
(15) promote + <u>tion</u> ⇨
promo<u>tion</u>
(16) divide + <u>sion</u> ⇨ divi<u>sion</u>
(17) comprehend + <u>sion</u> ⇨
comprehen<u>sion</u>
(18) attend + <u>tion</u> ⇨ atten<u>tion</u>
(19) compress + <u>ssion</u> ⇨
compre<u>ssion</u>
(20) insert + <u>tion</u> ⇨ inser<u>tion</u>
(21) diffuse + <u>sion</u> ⇨ diffu<u>sion</u>
(22) omit + <u>ssion</u> ⇨ omi<u>ssion</u>
(23) distort + <u>tion</u> ⇨ distor<u>tion</u>
(24) suspend + <u>sion</u> ⇨
suspen<u>sion</u>
(25) profess + <u>ssion</u> ⇨ profe<u>ssion</u>
(26) graduate + <u>tion</u> ⇨
gradua<u>tion</u>
(27) project + <u>tion</u> ⇨ projec<u>tion</u>
(28) devote + <u>tion</u> ⇨ devo<u>tion</u>
(29) contract + <u>tion</u> ⇨
contrac<u>tion</u>
(30) clinic + <u>cian</u> ⇨ clini<u>cian</u>
(31) prevent + <u>tion</u> ⇨ preven<u>tion</u>
(32) transmit + <u>ssion</u> ⇨
transmi<u>ssion</u>

(33) illustra<u>tion</u>
(34) opti<u>cian</u>
(35) impre<u>ssion</u>
(36) pollu<u>tion</u>
(37) admi<u>ssion</u>
(38) confu<u>sion</u>
(39) confe<u>ssion</u>
(40) indica<u>tion</u>
(41) excep<u>tion</u>
(42) permi<u>ssion</u>
(43) exhaus<u>tion</u>
(44) explo<u>sion</u>
(45) statisti<u>cian</u>
(46) inten<u>tion</u>
(47) accommoda<u>tion</u>
(48) diges<u>tion</u>
(49) intru<u>sion</u>
(50) deser<u>tion</u>
(51) emi<u>ssion</u>

UNIT 24

TEST 24.1

(1) ✓	**(8)** ✗	**(15)** ✓
(2) ✓	**(9)** ✗	**(16)** ✓
(3) ✓	**(10)** ✓	**(17)** ✗
(4) ✓	**(11)** ✓	**(18)** ✗
(5) ✓	**(12)** ✓	**(19)** ✓
(6) ✗	**(13)** ✓	**(20)** ✗
(7) ✓	**(14)** ✗	

(6) categories; (8) committee; (9) diffe<u>r</u>ence; (14) i<u>g</u>loo; (17) oc<u>c</u>ur; (18) prep<u>a</u>rations; (20) rhythms

TEST 24.2

(1) ✗	**(8)** ✓	**(15)** ✓
(2) ✓	**(9)** ✗	**(16)** ✗
(3) ✓	**(10)** ✓	**(17)** ✗
(4) ✓	**(11)** ✗	**(18)** ✗
(5) ✗	**(12)** ✓	**(19)** ✗
(6) ✓	**(13)** ✗	**(20)** ✗
(7) ✓	**(14)** ✓	

(1) autobiographi<u>es</u>; (5) conf<u>er</u>ence; (9) de<u>c</u>ision; (11) fishes'; (13) goose's; (16) o<u>x</u>; (17) privil<u>eg</u>e; (18) people's; (19) refe<u>r</u>ral; (20) suffe<u>r</u>ing

TEST 24.3

(1) ✗	**(8)** ✗	**(15)** ✓
(2) ✗	**(9)** ✗	**(16)** ✓
(3) ✓	**(10)** ✗	**(17)** ✗
(4) ✓	**(11)** ✓	**(18)** ✗
(5) ✗	**(12)** ✗	**(19)** ✗
(6) ✗	**(13)** ✓	**(20)** ✓
(7) ✗	**(14)** ✓	

(1) a<u>c</u>quit; (2) allegory; (5) comm<u>u</u>nicate; (6) contrac<u>tion</u>; (7) defe<u>rr</u>ed; (8) distill<u>er</u>y; (9) development; (10) elec<u>tion</u>; (12) glass<u>es</u>; (17) pilfe<u>r</u>ed; (18) phenome<u>n</u>on; (19) sunbur<u>n</u>ed

TEST 24.4

(1) ✗	**(9)** ✗	**(17)** ✓
(2) ✓	**(10)** ✗	**(18)** ✗
(3) ✗	**(11)** ✓	**(19)** ✗
(4) ✓	**(12)** ✓	**(20)** ✓
(5) ✓	**(13)** ✗	**(21)** ✓
(6) ✗	**(14)** ✗	**(22)** ✗
(7) ✓	**(15)** ✗	
(8) ✓	**(16)** ✗	

(1) accomm<u>o</u>dated; (3) confu<u>sion</u>; (6) discu<u>ssion</u>; (9) geese; (10) i<u>l</u>lustration; (13) mini<u>a</u>ture; (14) offe<u>r</u>ed; (15) pollu<u>tion</u>; (16) profe<u>ssion</u>; (18) suspen<u>sion</u>; (19) sugges<u>tion</u>; (22) tomat<u>o</u>

TEST 24.5

(1) ✗	**(9)** ✗	**(17)** ✓
(2) ✓	**(10)** ✓	**(18)** ✓
(3) ✗	**(11)** ✗	**(19)** ✗

(4) ✗	(12) ✗	(20) ✓	(3) ✗	(11) ✗	(19) ✗	(2) ✓	(10) ✓	(18) ✗
(5) ✓	(13) ✓	(21) ✓	(4) ✗	(12) ✓	(20) ✓	(3) ✗	(11) ✓	(19) ✓
(6) ✗	(14) ✗	(22) ✓	(5) ✗	(13) ✓	(21) ✗	(4) ✓	(12) ✗	(20) ✓
(7) ✓	(15) ✗		(6) ✗	(14) ✓	(22) ✓	(5) ✓	(13) ✓	(21) ✗
(8) ✓	(16) ✗		(7) ✓	(15) ✗		(6) ✗	(14) ✓	(22) ✗
			(8) ✓	(16) ✓		(7) ✗	(15) ✗	
						(8) ✓	(16) ✗	

(1) an*n*iversaries; *(3)* confer*r*ed; *(4)* children*'s*; *(6)* defer*e*nce; *(9)* igloo*s*; *(11)* overpop*u*late; *(12)* o*m*ission; *(14)* prefer*e*nce; *(15)* preferred; *(16)* refer*e*nce; *(19)* shipp*i*ng

(1) amat*e*urs; *(2)* beginner; *(3)* cliff*s*; *(4)* compres*s*ion; *(5)* disti*ll*eries; *(6)* exagger*a*ted; *(11)* prevention; *(15)* subeditor; *(19)* thi*ef*; *(21)* trans*m*ission

(3) bargai*n*ing; *(6)* de*s*ertion; *(7)* exh*au*stion; *(9)* firemen*'s*; *(12)* liabilit*i*es; *(15)* oa*s*es; *(16)* rhyth*m*; *(18)* sheep; *(21)* tomato*es*; *(22)* volcano*es*

TEST 24.6

(1) ✓	(9) ✓	(17) ✓
(2) ✗	(10) ✓	(18) ✗
(3) ✓	(11) ✓	(19) ✓
(4) ✗	(12) ✗	(20) ✓
(5) ✗	(13) ✓	(21) ✓
(6) ✓	(14) ✗	(22) ✗
(7) ✓	(15) ✓	
(8) ✗	(16) ✓	

(2) child*'s*; *(4)* cri*s*es; *(5)* dee*r*; *(8)* interfe*r*e; *(12)* pro*n*ounced; *(14)* series; *(18)* subcommi*tt*ee; *(22)* unfo*c*used

TEST 24.9

(1) ✓	(9) ✓	(17) ✗
(2) ✓	(10) ✗	(18) ✗
(3) ✗	(11) ✓	(19) ✓
(4) ✗	(12) ✗	(20) ✓
(5) ✗	(13) ✓	(21) ✓
(6) ✓	(14) ✓	(22) ✓
(7) ✗	(15) ✓	
(8) ✓	(16) ✗	

(3) communicator; *(4)* controversies; *(5)* differ*i*ng; *(7)* emitting; *(10)* feet; *(12)* infer*r*ed; *(16)* puppies*'*; *(17)* referend*u*m; *(18)* suffe*r*ed

TEST 24.12

(1) ✓	(9) ✓	(17) ✗
(2) ✗	(10) ✗	(18) ✓
(3) ✗	(11) ✓	(19) ✗
(4) ✗	(12) ✗	(20) ✗
(5) ✓	(13) ✓	(21) ✓
(6) ✗	(14) ✓	(22) ✗
(7) ✓	(15) ✓	
(8) ✗	(16) ✓	

(2) acqui*tt*ed; *(3)* antiseptic; *(4)* confer*r*ing; *(6)* diffu*s*ion; *(8)* eavesdropper; *(10)* forma*tt*ed; *(12)* infer*e*nce; *(17)* stati*st*ician; *(19)* swo*t*; *(20)* transfer*e*nce; *(22)* wives*'*

TEST 24.7

(1) ✓	(9) ✓	(17) ✓
(2) ✓	(10) ✗	(18) ✗
(3) ✓	(11) ✓	(19) ✓
(4) ✓	(12) ✗	(20) ✗
(5) ✗	(13) ✓	(21) ✗
(6) ✗	(14) ✓	(22) ✓
(7) ✗	(15) ✗	
(8) ✓	(16) ✗	

(5) distortion; *(6)* expres*s*ion; *(7)* gard*e*ner; *(10)* operation; *(12)* promotion; *(15)* subcons*c*ious; *(16)* subcategories; *(18)* septic; *(21)* who*s*e

TEST 24.10

(1) ✗	(9) ✗	(17) ✓
(2) ✓	(10) ✗	(18) ✗
(3) ✗	(11) ✓	(19) ✗
(4) ✓	(12) ✗	(20) ✓
(5) ✓	(13) ✓	(21) ✓
(6) ✗	(14) ✓	(22) ✓
(7) ✓	(15) ✗	
(8) ✗	(16) ✗	

(1) alleg*o*ries; *(3)* avocad*os*; *(6)* cri*s*is; *(8)* deferral; *(9)* exception; *(10)* forg*o*tten; *(12)* ibises; *(15)* offering; *(16)* opti*c*ian; *(18)* pilfering; *(19)* strum*m*ed

TEST 24.11

(1) ✓	(9) ✗	(17) ✓

TEST 24.8

(1) ✗	(9) ✓	(17) ✓
(2) ✗	(10) ✓	(18) ✓

(1) interested; superb
(2) antic; comet
(3) discos; preen
(4) counter; relative
(5) inner; mister
(6) comma; coining
(7) proudly; reedy
(8) imagine; prowler
(9) antique; unit
(10) comely; condor
(11) under; profiterole
(12) interred; prodigy
(13) mistletoe; interim
(14) intern; properly
(15) conical; probing

(16) imperceptible

(17) <u>un</u>professional
(18) <u>in</u>accessible
(19) <u>dis</u>advantage
(20) <u>un</u>compromising
(21) <u>in</u>considerate
(22) <u>un</u>characteristic
(23) <u>ir</u>replaceable
(24) <u>dis</u>belief
(25) <u>un</u>bearable
(26) <u>un</u>insured
(27) <u>in</u>animate
(28) <u>in</u>eligible
(29) <u>ir</u>reconcilable
(30) <u>dis</u>regarded
(31) <u>un</u>patriotic
(32) <u>in</u>appropriate
(33) <u>un</u>remarkable
(34) <u>in</u>effective

UNIT 26

(1) - (10) *The 10 incorrectly spelt words and their correct spellings are as follows:*
distur<u>b</u>ence ⇨ distur<u>b</u><u>a</u>nce
<u>in</u>acknowledged ⇨ <u>un</u>acknowledged
improb<u>i</u>bly ⇨ improb<u>a</u>bly
<u>un</u>relevance ⇨ <u>ir</u>relevance
<u>dis</u>diagnose ⇨ <u>mis</u>diagnose
<u>mis</u>approvingly ⇨ <u>dis</u>approvingly
<u>in</u>drinkable ⇨ <u>un</u>drinkable
<u>ree</u>valuation ⇨ <u>re-e</u>valuation
<u>un</u>admiss<u>a</u>ble ⇨ <u>in</u>admiss<u>i</u>ble
<u>in</u>personated ⇨ <u>im</u>personated

(11) irreparable
(12) indefinable OR undefinable
(13) inexperience
(14) encouragement
(15) proficiency
(16) irreverent
(17) misgovernment
(18) disagreement
(19) inconsistent OR inconsistency
(20) disrespectful
(21) reassurance
(22) imprudence
(23) unemployment
(24) irretrievable

(25) <u>jab</u> + <u>ed</u> ⇨ jabbed
(26) <u>president</u> + <u>tial</u> ⇨ presidential
(27) <u>induce</u> + <u>ible</u> ⇨ inducible
(28) <u>guide</u> + <u>ance</u> ⇨ guidance
(29) <u>differ</u> + <u>ed</u> ⇨ differed
(30) <u>irritate</u> + <u>tion</u> ⇨ irritation
(31) <u>urge</u> + <u>ency</u> ⇨ urgency
(32) <u>obsess</u> + <u>ssion</u> ⇨ obsession
(33) <u>chisel</u> + <u>ing</u> ⇨ chiselling
(34) <u>comply</u> + <u>ant</u> ⇨ compliant
(35) <u>invent</u> + <u>tion</u> ⇨ invention
(36) <u>hysterical</u> + <u>ly</u> ⇨ hysterically OR <u>hysteric</u> + <u>ally</u> ⇨ hysterically
(37) <u>persuade</u> + <u>sion</u> ⇨ persuasion
(38) <u>rhetoric</u> + <u>cian</u> ⇨ rhetorician
(39) <u>able</u> + <u>ly</u> ⇨ ably
(40) <u>plod</u> + <u>er</u> ⇨ plodder
(41) <u>transfer</u> + <u>ing</u> ⇨ transferring
(42) <u>erode</u> + <u>sion</u> ⇨ erosion
(43) <u>eerie</u> + <u>ly</u> ⇨ eerily
(44) <u>trek</u> + <u>ed</u> ⇨ trekked
(45) <u>classify</u> + <u>able</u> ⇨ classifiable
(46) <u>idealistic</u> + <u>ally</u> ⇨ idealistically
(47) <u>conscience</u> + <u>tious</u> ⇨ conscientious
(48) <u>transgress</u> + <u>ssion</u> ⇨ transgression
(49) <u>absorb</u> + <u>ent</u> ⇨ absorbent
(50) <u>forensic</u> + <u>ally</u> ⇨ forensically
(51) <u>consequent</u> + <u>tial</u> ⇨ consequential
(52) <u>occupy</u> + <u>ancy</u> ⇨ occupancy
(53) <u>cohere</u> + <u>ence</u> ⇨ coherence
(54) <u>flog</u> + <u>ing</u> ⇨ flogging
(55) <u>complete</u> + <u>tion</u> ⇨ completion
(56) <u>success</u> + <u>ssion</u> ⇨ succession

UNIT 27

(1) ours
(2) boss
(3) thief
(4) chiefs
(5) complex
(6) echoes
(7) bookworm
(8) theirs
(9) anchovy
(10) alleys
(11) mattress
(12) puffs
(13) rhinoceroses OR rhinoceros
(14) myself
(15) handkerchiefs
(16) advice
(17) giraffes
(18) moose
(19) barracks
(20) lampshade
(21) matchstick
(22) commandos OR commandoes
(23) index
(24) beliefs
(25) ally
(26) torpedoes OR torpedos
(27) yours
(28) confectioneries
(29) offspring
(30) axe
(31) zeros
(32) archipelagos OR archipelagoes

(33) bis<u>ons</u> ✗ ⇨ bis<u>on</u>
(34) information<u>s</u> ✗ ⇨ information
(35) cargo<u>es'</u> ✗ ⇨ cargo<u>es</u> OR cargos
(36) roof<u>'s</u> ✗ ⇨ roof<u>s</u>
(37) bookshel<u>fs</u> ✗ ⇨ bookshel<u>ves</u>
(38) oboe<u>s's</u> ✗ ⇨ oboe<u>s'</u>
(39) potat<u>os</u> ✗ ⇨ potat<u>oes</u>
(40) waltz<u>es'</u> ✗ ⇨ waltz<u>es</u>
(41) dragon<u>s's</u> ✗ ⇨ dragon<u>s'</u>
(42) Mosquito<u>s</u> ✗ ⇨ Mosquit<u>oes'</u> OR Mosquitos' OR Mosquit<u>o</u>
(43) your<u>s'</u> ✗ ⇨ your<u>s</u>
(44) hoax<u>'s</u> ✗ ⇨ hoax<u>es</u>

UNIT 28

(1) d <u>r</u> <u>a</u> <u>k</u> <u>e</u>
(2) d <u>u</u> <u>c</u> <u>k</u>
(3) r <u>o</u> <u>o</u> <u>s</u> <u>t</u> <u>e</u> <u>r</u>
(4) h <u>e</u> <u>n</u>
(5) g <u>a</u> <u>n</u> <u>d</u> <u>e</u> <u>r</u>
(6) g <u>o</u> <u>o</u> <u>s</u> <u>e</u>
(7) b <u>o</u> <u>a</u> r
(8) s <u>o</u> w
(9) r <u>a</u> <u>m</u>
(10) e <u>w</u> e
(11) t <u>o</u> <u>m</u>
(12) t <u>i</u> <u>g</u> <u>r</u> <u>e</u> <u>s</u> <u>s</u>

(13) d r o n e
(14) s t a g
(15) v i x e n
(16) p e a h e n
(17) b u l l
(18) c o w

(19) duchess
(20) bridegroom OR groom
(21) heiress
(22) lord
(23) shepherd
(24) daughter
(25) waiter
(26) sister
(27) abbess
(28) maidservant
(29) hero
(30) stewardess
(31) Mrs
(32) lass
(33) prince
(34) master
(35) countess
(36) headmistress
(37) goddess
(38) empress
(39) sir
(40) actress
(41) sire
(42) sultana
(43) wizard OR warlock
(44) widower
(45) nun
(46) spinster
(47) aunt
(48) marchioness
(49) fiancé
(50) billy goat

UNIT 29

(1) pact
(2) imminent
(3) we're
(4) arms
(5) bazaar
(6) mettle
(7) oral
(8) foreword
(9) quarts
(10) borne
(11) wreak
(12) swot

(13) coarse
(14) troop
(15) stake
(16) duel
(17) sought
(18) naval
(19) cast
(20) where
(21) guerrilla
(22) suite
(23) tolled
(24) hail
(25) whine
(26) mowed
(27) lava
(28) gilt
(29) their
(30) lone
(31) counsel
(32) borders
(33) horde
(34) lessen
(35) ads
(36) Fates
(37) laps
(38) hangers
(39) peel
(40) whet
(41) storey

UNIT 30

TEST 30.1

(1) ✗	**(8)** ✓	**(15)** ✗
(2) ✗	**(9)** ✗	**(16)** ✗
(3) ✗	**(10)** ✓	**(17)** ✓
(4) ✗	**(11)** ✗	**(18)** ✓
(5) ✓	**(12)** ✓	**(19)** ✗
(6) ✓	**(13)** ✗	**(20)** ✓
(7) ✗	**(14)** ✗	

(1) abbot; **(2)** bizarre; **(3)** compliant; **(4)** cargoes; **(7)** empress; **(9)** forward; **(11)** headmaster; **(13)** imminent; **(14)** increase **(15)** inconsistent; **(16)** indices; **(19)** offspring

TEST 30.2

(1) ✓	**(8)** ✗	**(15)** ✓
(2) ✓	**(9)** ✓	**(16)** ✓

(3) ✗ **(10)** ✓ **(17)** ✗
(4) ✗ **(11)** ✗ **(18)** ✓
(5) ✗ **(12)** ✓ **(19)** ✗
(6) ✗ **(13)** ✓ **(20)** ✗
(7) ✓ **(14)** ✗

(3) calypsos; **(4)** disagreement; **(5)** discolour; **(6)** drone; **(8)** handkerchiefs; **(11)** information; **(14)** llama; **(17)** aural; **(19)** quarts; **(20)** reallocated

TEST 30.3

(1) ✓	**(8)** ✓	**(15)** ✓
(2) ✓	**(9)** ✗	**(16)** ✓
(3) ✓	**(10)** ✗	**(17)** ✗
(4) ✗	**(11)** ✗	**(18)** ✗
(5) ✓	**(12)** ✓	**(19)** ✓
(6) ✓	**(13)** ✓	**(20)** ✗
(7) ✗	**(14)** ✗	

(4) consequential; **(7)** duchess; **(9)** heiress; **(10)** ill-advised; **(11)** imperceptible; **(14)** marquis; **(17)** occupancy; **(20)** redoubling

TEST 30.4

(1) ✗	**(9)** ✓	**(17)** ✗
(2) ✓	**(10)** ✗	**(18)** ✓
(3) ✗	**(11)** ✗	**(19)** ✗
(4) ✓	**(12)** ✓	**(20)** ✓
(5) ✓	**(13)** ✓	**(21)** ✗
(6) ✓	**(14)** ✓	**(22)** ✓
(7) ✗	**(15)** ✓	
(8) ✗	**(16)** ✓	

(1) ably; **(3)** completion; **(4)** commandoes; **(7)** eerily; **(8)** gorilla; **(10)** improper; **(11)** inaccessible; **(17)** reassurance; **(19)** barracks; **(21)** their

TEST 30.5

(1) ✓	**(9)** ✗	**(17)** ✓
(2) ✓	**(10)** ✓	**(18)** ✗
(3) ✗	**(11)** ✗	**(19)** ✓

(4) ✓ (12) × (20) ✓
(5) ✓ (13) ✓ (21) ×
(6) × (14) × (22) ✓
(7) × (15) ✓
(8) ✓ (16) ✓

(3) chiselling; *(6)* echoes; *(7)* fiancée; *(9)* inadmissible; *(11)* irreconcilable; *(12)* luxuries; *(14)* navel; *(18)* spinster; *(21)* uninsured

TEST 30.6

(1) ✓ (9) ✓ (17) ✓
(2) × (10) ✓ (18) ✓
(3) ✓ (11) × (19) ✓
(4) ✓ (12) ✓ (20) ✓
(5) × (13) ✓ (21) ×
(6) ✓ (14) × (22) ×
(7) ✓ (15) ×
(8) × (16) ×

(2) council; *(5)* disapprovingly; *(8)* impersonated; *(11)* irredeemable; *(14)* ourselves; *(15)* profess; *(16)* re-evaluation; *(21)* unprofessional; *(22)* urgency

TEST 30.7

(1) × (9) ✓ (17) ✓
(2) ✓ (10) × (18) ×
(3) ✓ (11) × (19) ×
(4) ✓ (12) ✓ (20) ✓
(5) ✓ (13) ✓ (21) ×
(6) ✓ (14) ✓ (22) ✓
(7) ✓ (15) ×
(8) ✓ (16) ✓

(1) anchovies; *(10)* irrelevance; *(11)* irreverent; *(15)* rhythms; *(18)* troupe; *(19)* uninterested; *(21)* waitress

TEST 30.8

(1) ✓ (9) × (17) ×
(2) ✓ (10) × (18) ×

(3) ✓ (11) × (19) ✓
(4) ✓ (12) ✓ (20) ✓
(5) ✓ (13) ✓ (21) ×
(6) ✓ (14) × (22) ✓
(7) × (15) ✓
(8) ✓ (16) ✓

(7) goddess; *(9)* imprisonment; *(10)* inappropriate; *(11)* inconsistency; *(14)* obsession; *(17)* they're; *(18)* thieves; *(21)* unemployment

TEST 30.9

(1) × (9) × (17) ×
(2) ✓ (10) × (18) ✓
(3) ✓ (11) ✓ (19) ✓
(4) × (12) × (20) ✓
(5) ✓ (13) ✓ (21) ✓
(6) ✓ (14) × (22) ✓
(7) × (15) ✓
(8) × (16) ×

(1) absorbent; *(4)* dissatisfied; *(7)* extracurricular; *(8)* forward; *(9)* guidance; *(10)* encouragement; *(12)* irritation; *(14)* mouths; *(16)* suite; *(17)* steward

TEST 30.10

(1) ✓ (9) × (17) ×
(2) ✓ (10) × (18) ✓
(3) ✓ (11) × (19) ×
(4) × (12) × (20) ×
(5) ✓ (13) ✓ (21) ×
(6) ✓ (14) ✓ (22) ✓
(7) × (15) ×
(8) ✓ (16) ×

(4) bosses; *(7)* disturbance; *(9)* hoard; *(10)* ineligible; *(11)* insignificance; *(12)* irreplaceable; *(15)* misremembered; *(16)* perceptible; *(17)* rhinoceroses; *(19)* trekked; *(20)* unremarkably; *(21)* unpatriotic

TEST 30.11

(1) × (9) ✓ (17) ✓
(2) ✓ (10) × (18) ×
(3) × (11) × (19) ×
(4) ✓ (12) ✓ (20) ×
(5) × (13) ✓ (21) ×
(6) × (14) ✓ (22) ×
(7) ✓ (15) ×
(8) ✓ (16) ×

(1) autonomous; *(3)* coherence; *(5)* disrespectful; *(6)* flogging; *(10)* imprudence; *(11)* mosquito; *(15)* theirs; *(16)* transferring; *(18)* ungrammatical; *(19)* unrepentant; *(20)* unresolvable; *(21)* waltzes; *(22)* wreak

TEST 30.12

(1) ✓ (9) × (17) ×
(2) × (10) ✓ (18) ✓
(3) × (11) ✓ (19) ✓
(4) ✓ (12) ✓ (20) ×
(5) ✓ (13) × (21) ✓
(6) × (14) × (22) ×
(7) × (15) ×
(8) × (16) ✓

(2) bachelor; *(3)* confectionery; *(6)* disoriented; *(7)* erosion; *(8)* extraterrestrial; *(9)* fêtes; *(13)* proficiency; *(14)* rhetorician; *(15)* shepherdess; *(17)* supersede; *(20)* uncompromising; *(22)* zeros

UNIT 1

tomorrow
forty
criticises
identity
variety
probably
awkward
occupied
developing
familiar
relevant
amateur
harassed
definite
twelfth
Wednesday
attached
category
bruised
wonderful

accident
occasion
cemetery
parliament
recognise
dictionary
sincere
determined
explanation
signature
queue
embarrass
programme
community
competition
guarantee
vehicle
physical
correspond
eight
neighbour
accompany
secretary

yacht
available

necessary
government
pronunciation
temperature
according
vegetable
individual
restaurant
excellent

disappear
strength
build
medicine
exercise
group
circle
straight
address
calendar
separate
ordinary
fruit
imagine
particular
height
learn
recent
natural
favourite
often
quarter
actually
through
thorough
strange
surprise
popular
remember
breathe
consider
decide
certain
perhaps
purpose
century
interest
important
therefore
sentence
grammar

desperate
earth

controversy
determination
interrupted
recommend
curiosity
sacrifice
prejudice
February
desperately
committee
accompaniment
argument
eighth
languages
occurrences
communication
environment
actual
sincerity

ancient
system
diligent
aggressive
shoulder
centre
knowledge
convenience
rhythm
average
complete
accidentally
especially
peculiar
continue
existence
opportunity
detached
describe
equipment
frequently
sincerely
possession
minute
experiment
experience
expertise
develop
soldier
possible
parallel

history
guard
naughty
material
forwards
mention
bicycle
appear
library
extreme
suppose
rhyme
length
thought

woman
breath
questions
difficult
increase
busy
arrive
early
guide
promised
enough
pressure
notice
opposite
regular
occasionally
positions
though

UNIT 2

reincarnation
coincide
anti-inflammatory
co-operation
reimburse
collaborate
de-emphasise
deduce
antihero
anti-hero
re-employ
recurring
semicircle
reduce
collision
redeem

re-enter

co-ordination
semiautomatic
semi-automatic
redesigned
microbiologist
de-escalate
re-editing
antibodies
co-organisers
semicolon
demoted
re-examining
antisocial
re-elected
co-operate
micro-organism

friend
leisure
anxiety
convenient
reign
freight
foreign
eiderdown
impatient
briefcase
weight
neighbourhood
yield
reindeer
sovereign
hygiene
gondolier

quiet
relieved
seized
besieged
counterfeit
eighteenth
unveiling
ingredient
reins
lenient
grieved
died
brigadier
lieutenant
pieces
chandelier
believe

aliens
niece
disobedient
poltergeist
weird
scientific
well-received
decaffeinated
beige

cautious
tiptoed
vicious
defenceless
sailor
precious
nutritious
unappetising
boring
repetitious
nonsense
fictitious
ambitious
monotonous
spacious
luxurious
voracious
atrocious

delicious
malicious
curious
famous
various
poisonous
anxious
suspicious
adventurous
superstitious
barbarous
hideous
mountainous
dangerous
perilous
humongous
conscious
hazardous
infamous
luscious
marvellous
tremendous
outrageous

jealous
precarious
precipitous
precocious
tedious
joyous
glamorous
gracious
infectious
anonymous
vigorous
treacherous
venomous
ridiculous
thunderous
herbivorous
fabulous
disastrous
pretentious
prosperous
rebellious
stupendous

essential
confidential
artificial
officials
provincial
special
residential
glacial
social
infomercials

superficial
financial
partial
commercial
potential
sequential
racial
palatial
crucial
influential
especial
martial
impartial
facial
unofficial
beneficial
judicial
substantial

courage
discourage
lead
mislead
relevant
irrelevant
behave
misbehave
possess
dispossess
print
misprint
address
misaddress
regular
irregular
obey
disobey
govern
misgovern
legal
illegal
count
discount
miscount
agree
disagree
guide
misguide
heard
misheard
appoint
disappoint
legible
illegible
rational
irrational
allow
disallow
regard
disregard
misregard
pose
dispose
fit
misfit
shaped
misshaped
arm
disarm
able
disable

align
misalign
conduct
misconduct
card
discard
grace
disgrace
honest
dishonest
handle
mishandle
label
mislabel

illiterate
disapproval
misspelled
misspelt
irresponsible
disappearance
misremember
dissatisfied
discontinuing
mistreatment
disadvantage
disagreeable
illogical
mistrustful
irresistible
disappointment
misapprehension
misdeed
irreversible
mislaid
disembarked
discourteous
misdirection
disassemble
discomfort
misinformation
disenchanted
misconception
dissimilarity
misapplied
disruption
misspeak
disorderly
misjudged
dismissal
illegitimate
disbelievingly

conceive
mischievous
conscience
species
ceiling
achievement
nuclei
societies
juiciest
concierge
piecemeal
receipts
glacier
financier
piercingly
deceivers
recipes
deficiency
omniscient
transceivers
conceitedness
unperceived

scheme
chorus
charity
anarchy
crypt
calypso
lyric
psyche
mascot
crescent
cascade
fiasco
cyanide
photosynthesis
syndicate
synonym
Achilles
bronchitis
enchilada
monarchy
symbol
rye
typical
symptom
martyr
sty
pyre

typhoon
obscene
adolescent
scimitar
crescendo
chided
urchins
archipelago
besmirched
gymkhana
gyroscope
hymn
gymnasium
hibiscus
escapade
fresco
fluorescent

asymmetrical
charismatic
schemes
isosceles
cyclists
orchestra
echoing
chrysanthemums
scenery
platypus
effervescent
architect
susceptible
sceptre
chameleon
tympani
character
scholar
hierarchical

chef
tongue
moustache
unique
machine
league
brochure
parachute
chalet
antique
colleagues
boutique
plague
chivalry
bouquet
chandelier

catalogue
pistachio
cheque

picturesque
consequence
quest
squeak
bewitch
challenge
archer
champagne
banquet
racquet
prequel
squelch
query
aqueduct
physique
queasy
orchid
chlorine
stomach
fuchsia
request
grotesque
squeeze
frequent
arachnid
chaperone
machete
chivalrous
technique
mosque
question
plaque
avalanche
crochet
crèche
archive
chic
chasm
chauffeur
charade
bequeath
equestrian
querulous
opaque

democratic
democratically
separate

separately
harsh
harshly
grave
gravely
begrudging
begrudgingly
literal
literally
flimsy
flimsily
magic
magically
naive
naively
persuasive
persuasively
complete
completely
abominable
abominably
ready
readily
historic
historically
ordinary
ordinarily
precise
precisely
cryptic
cryptically
hoarse
hoarsely
environment
environmentally

miserably
basically
immediately
cheerily
inexplicably
pompously
academically
temporarily
tangibly
elaborately

UNIT 11

prevent
preventable
envy
enviable
apply

applicable
mention
mentionable
adore
adorable
question
questionable
admit
admissible
reverse
reversible
like
likeable
answer
answerable
construct
constructable
constructible
imagine
imaginable
deny
deniable
attach
attachable
deduce
deducible
regret
regrettable
knowledge
knowledgeable
recommend
recommendable
programme
programmable
achieve
achievable
vary
variable
access
accessible
breathe
breathable
suggest
suggestible
collapse
collapsible
destruct
destructible
tolerate
tolerable
suppose
supposable
divide
divisible

consume
consumable
collect
collectible
appreciate
appreciable

conclusion
debatable
damage
considerably
suggestion
sensibly
comfortable
purchase
legible
impossible
reliable
changeable
forcible
persuadable
dependably
enjoyable
noticeably
understandable

UNIT 13

mature
immature
attentive
inattentive
correct
incorrect
balance
imbalance
advisable
inadvisable
mortal
immortal
patient
impatient
definite
indefinite
prudent
imprudent
famous
infamous
adequate
inadequate
practical
impractical
sufficient
insufficient

precise
imprecise
justice
injustice
valid
invalid
moral
immoral
edible
inedible
moveable
immoveable

interview
review
immigrate
indirect
redirect
innovate
renovate
implied
replied
retake
intake
rejected
injected
interjected
interplay
replay
infused
refused
intersects
insects
reformed
informed
imported
reported
reconnect
interconnect
impelled
repelled
reactive
inactive
intermediate
immediate
incur
recur
repaired
impaired
inclined
reclined

national
international

decorate
redecorate
prove
improve
humane
inhumane
accurate
inaccurate
act
react
interact
claim
reclaim
change
interchange
polite
impolite
acquaint
reacquaint
formal
informal
city
intercity
plant
implant
replant
library
interlibrary
fund
refund
consider
reconsider
destructible
indestructible
personal
impersonal
interpersonal
mission
remission
intermission
capable
incapable
dignity
indignity
boot
reboot
mobile
immobile
compatible
incompatible
twine
intertwine
generate
regenerate

separable
inseparable
plausible
implausible
material
immaterial
galactic
intergalactic
conclusive
inconclusive
pertinent
impertinent

rough
tough
ruff
cough
doubt
drought
route
clout
foe
tow
dough
vow
trout
bought
wart
fraught
thorough
duller
cower
colour
trough
plough
bough
thou
ewe
true
through
rogue
thought
naught
draught
wrought
hour
flower
borough
sour
nought
caught
quart

chart
south
sought
sort
fort
fought
pout
taut
taught
throughout
nowt
gout
throat
bellow
furlough
sallow
allow
bout
ought
thwart
distraught
although
below
hiccough
woe

doubts
muscle
island
biscuits
lamb
vehicles
business
solemnly
succumbed
thistle
cologne

fascinated
archaeologist
nuisance
queued
wrinkled
scent
wreck
rhymes
receipt
rustling
chemicals
guarantees
gnashed
pneumonia

disguise
debt
knapsack
campaigning
catacombs

observe
observant
observance
differ
different
difference
hinder
hindrance
obey
obedient
obedience
hesitate
hesitant
hesitancy
hesitance
expect
expectant
expectancy
expectance
reside
resident
residence
residency
assist
assistant
assistance
correspond
correspondent
correspondence
suffice
sufficient
sufficiency
survey
surveillance
depend
dependant
dependent
dependence
dependency

increment
efficiency
innocent
substance
decency
tolerance

independent
confident
frequency
insistent
persistent
disobedience
assurances
negligent
recipient
eloquence
brilliance
defiant
endurance
resilience
component
coherent
competent
malevolent
lenience
sentences
inefficiency
apparent
incompetence

altar
alter
draught
draft
practice
practise
guest
guessed
morning
mourning
steel
steal
who's
whose
bruise
brews
heart
hart
accept
except
principle
principal
stationery
stationary
led
lead
ball
bawl

great
grate
wary
weary
device
devise
cereal
serial
ascent
assent
further
farther
bridal
bridle
prophet
profit
affect
effect
herd
heard
desert
dessert
compliments
complements
aisle
isle
proceed
precede
lightning
lightening
meddle
medal
license
licence
past
passed
aloud
allowed
descent
dissent
prophecy
prophesy
missed
mist
weather
whether
advice
advise
currant
current
patients
patience
wrung
rung

market
supermarket
committee
subcommittee
septic
antiseptic
categories
subcategories
stars
superstars
graph
autograph
conscious
subconscious
climax
anticlimax
marine
submarine
biographies
autobiographies

clockwise
anticlockwise
natural
supernatural
title
subtitle
human
superhuman
tract
subtract
theft
antitheft
anti-theft
man
superman
merged
submerged
mobiles
automobiles
glue
superglue
biotic
antibiotic
imposed
superimposed
divided
subdivided
way
subway
heading
subheading

computers
supercomputers
editor
subeditor

girl
girls
knave
knaves
tomato
tomatoes
celebration
celebrations
woman
women
mouse
mice
ibis
ibises
anniversary
anniversaries
foot
feet
man
men
sheep (singular)
sheep (plural)
privilege
privileges
rhythm
rhythms
ox
oxen
igloo
igloos
child
children
tooth
teeth
goose
geese
distillery
distilleries
attendee
attendees
fox
foxes
this
these
miniature
miniatures
wife

wives
cactus
cactuses
cacti
liability
liabilities
louse
lice
volcano
volcanoes
volcanos
allegory
allegories
loaf
loaves
crisis
crises
deer (singular)
deer (plural)
that
those
phenomenon
phenomena

children's
soldiers'
fishes
glasses
shoes'
controversies
scarves
amateurs'
firemen's
cookies
radios'
people's
cliffs
fungi
avocados
quizzes'
oases
puppies'
series
hippopotamuses

begin
beginner
garden
gardener
communicate
communicator
forget

forgotten
limit
limitation
equip
equipped
sunburn
sunburnt
sunburned
ship
shipping
occur
occurring
nag
nagging
prepare
preparations
acquit
acquitted
engine
engineer
bargain
bargaining
overpopulate
overpopulation
babysit
babysitter
shoulder
shouldered
strum
strummed
carry
carrier

accommodated
insuring
formatted
emitting
unfocused
embarrassment
development
eavesdropper
pronounced
exaggerated

conference
deferral
difference
suffered
offered
inferred
surfing
reference

referral
preference
differing
conferred
referendum
transference
pilfering
refereed

deference
conferring
deferred
offering
inference
pilfered
suffering
surfer
preferred
interfere

music
musician
commit
commission
decide
decision
educate
education
discuss
discussion
adopt
adoption
include
inclusion
operate
operation
suggest
suggestion
electric
electrician
predict
prediction
express
expression
submit
submission
elect
election
promote
promotion
divide
division

comprehend
comprehension
attend
attention
compress
compression
insert
insertion
diffuse
diffusion
omit
omission
distort
distortion
suspend
suspension
profess
profession
graduate
graduation
project
projection
devote
devotion
contract
contraction
clinic
clinician
prevent
prevention
transmit
transmission

illustrate
illustration
optic
optician
impress
impression
pollute
pollution
admit
admission
confuse
confusion
confess
confession
indicate
indication
except
exception
permit
permission
exhaust

exhaustion
explode
explosion
statistic
statistician
intend
intention
accommodate
accommodation
digest
digestion
intrude
intrusion
desert
desertion
emit
emission

supervision
interested
disarm
inaudible
superb
antic
miscalculate
ill-advised
comet
expose
contract
profess
discos
preen
extraordinary
counter
unabridged
relative
reapplied
misfire
increase
inner
ungrammatical
prologue
mister
rebuilt
comma
discolour
coining
exclude
pronoun
extraterrestrial
proudly
reedy

intervene
imagine
autonomous
extract
dishonour
prowler
unrepentant
antique
indistinct
unit
misplaced
comely
convert
redeliver
condor
disown
unresolvable
inequality
under
profiterole
proactive
interred
disqualify
refill
exclaim
prodigy
subcontinent
mistletoe
misremembered
external
interim
inhibit
supersede
intern
properly
dissatisfied
conical
insignificance
misdial
probing
extracurricular
extra-curricular

perceptible
imperceptible
professional
unprofessional
accessible
inaccessible
advantage
disadvantage
compromising
uncompromising
considerate

inconsiderate
characteristic
uncharacteristic
replaceable
irreplaceable
belief
disbelief
bearable
unbearable
insured
uninsured
animate
inanimate
eligible
ineligible
reconcilable
irreconcilable
regarded
disregarded
patriotic
unpatriotic
appropriate
inappropriate
remarkable
unremarkable
effective
ineffective

uninterested
discontinued
disturbance
unacknowledged
improper
improbably
irredeemable
interlaced
unfashionable
irrelevance
imprisonment
reallocated
subdivision
misdiagnose
disapprovingly
undrinkable
re-evaluation
inadmissible
redoubling
unadvertised
subscript
uninvited
automatic
impersonated

disoriented

irreparable
indefinable
undefinable
inexperience
encouragement
proficiency
irreverent
misgovernment
disagreement
inconsistent
inconsistency
disrespectful
reassurance
imprudence
unemployment
irretrievable

jab
jabbed
president
presidential
induce
inducible
guide
guidance
differ
differed
irritate
irritation
urge
urgency
obsess
obsession
chisel
chiselling
comply
compliant
invent
invention
hysteric
hysterical
hysterically
persuade
persuasion
rhetoric
rhetorician
able
ably
plod
plodder
transfer
transferring

erode
erosion
eerie
eerily
trek
trekked
classify
classifiable
idealistic
idealistically
conscience
conscientious
transgress
transgression
absorb
absorbent
forensic
forensically
consequent
consequential
occupy
occupancy
cohere
coherence
flog
flogging
complete
completion
success
succession

mine
ours
boss
bosses
thief
thieves
chief
chiefs
complex
complexes
echo
echoes
bookworm
bookworms
his
theirs
anchovy
anchovies
alley
alleys
mattress

mattresses
puff
puffs
rhinoceros (singular)
rhinoceros (plural)
rhinoceroses
myself
ourselves
handkerchief
handkerchiefs
advice (singular)
advice (plural)
giraffe
giraffes
moose (singular)
moose (plural)
barracks (singular)
barracks (plural)
lampshade
lampshades
matchstick
matchsticks
commando
commandos
commandoes
index
indices
belief
beliefs
ally
allies
torpedo
torpedoes
torpedos
yours (singular)
yours (plural)
confectionery
confectioneries
offspring (singular)
offspring (plural)
axe
axes
zero (singular noun)
zeros (plural noun)
archipelago
archipelagos
archipelagoes

animals
snakes
bison (plural)
lions
tigers
llamas

pictures
information
planets
ships
cargoes
cargos
luxuries
docks
roofs
cottages
tiles
years
spines
bookshelves
house's
oboes'
crescendos
hairs
chef's
carrots
potatoes
radishes
leeks
rhythms
tangos
calypsos
waltzes
flames
dragons'
nostrils
mouths
mosquitoes'
mosquitos'
mosquito
bites
shoes
yours
clothes
chairs
gnomes
hoaxes
fairies'
children

drake
duck
rooster
hen
gander
goose
boar
sow

ram
ewe
tom
tigress
drone
stag
vixen
peahen
bull
cow

duke
duchess
bridegroom
groom
bride
heir
heiress
lord
lady
shepherd
shepherdess
son
daughter
waiter
waitress
brother
sister
abbot
abbess
manservant
maidservant
hero
heroine
steward
stewardess
Mr
Mrs
lad
lass
prince
princess
master
mistress
earl
countess
headmaster
headmistress
god
goddess
emperor
empress
sir
madam

actor
actress
sire
dam
sultan
sultana
wizard
warlock
witch
widower
widow
monk
nun
bachelor
spinster
uncle
aunt
marquis
marchioness
fiancé
fiancée
billy goat
nanny goat

UNIT 29

pact
packed
eminent
imminent
were
we're
alms
arms
bazaar
bizarre
metal
mettle
aural
oral
foreword
forward
quartz
quarts
born
borne
reek
wreak
swot
swat
course
coarse
troop
troupe

steak
stake
duel
dual
sort
sought
naval
navel
cast
caste
wear
where
gorilla
guerrilla
suite
sweet
told
tolled
hale
hail
whine
wine
mowed
mode
lava
larva
guilt
gilt
they're
their
lone
loan
council
counsel
borders
boarders
hoard
horde
lessen
lesson
ads
adds
fêtes
Fates
laps
lapse
hangars
hangers
peel
peal
whet
wet
storey
story

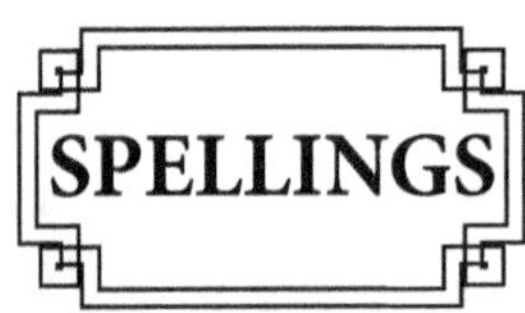

SPELLINGS

*As noted at the start of this book, all the words in **bold** in this section are those that are contained in the government's **statutory word lists** for Years 3 & 4 and Years 5 & 6.*

abbess
abbot
able
ably
abominable
abominably
absorb
absorbent
academically
accept
access
accessible
accident
accidentally
accommodate
accommodated
accommodation
accompaniment
accompany
according
accurate
achievable
achieve
achievement
Achilles
acquaint
acquit
acquitted
act
actor
actress
actual
actually
address
adds
adequate
admissible
admission
admit
adolescent
adopt

adoption
adorable
adore
ads
advantage
adventurous
advice (plural)
advice (singular)
advisable
advise
affect
aggressive
agree
aisle
aliens
align
allegories
allegory
alley
alleys
allies
allow
allowed
ally
alms
aloud
altar
alter
although
amateur
amateurs'
ambitious
anarchy
anchovies
anchovy
ancient
animals
animate
anniversaries
anniversary
anonymous
answer
answerable
anti-hero
anti-inflammatory
anti-theft
antibiotic
antibodies
antic
anticlimax
anticlockwise
antihero
antique
antiseptic

antisocial
antitheft
anxiety
anxious
apparent
appear
applicable
apply
appoint
appreciable
appreciate
appropriate
aqueduct
arachnid
archaeologist
archer
archipelago
archipelagoes
archipelagos
architect
archive
argument
arm
arms
arrive
artificial
ascent
assent
assist
assistance
assistant
assurances
asymmetrical
atrocious
attach
attachable
attached
attend
attendee
attendees
attention
attentive
aunt
aural
autobiographies
autograph
automatic
automobiles
autonomous
available
avalanche
average
avocados
awkward

axe
axes

babysit
babysitter
bachelor
balance
ball
banquet
barbarous
bargain
bargaining
barracks (plural)
barracks (singular)
basically
bawl
bazaar
bearable
begin
beginner
begrudging
begrudgingly
behave
beige
belief
beliefs
believe
bellow
below
beneficial
bequeath
besieged
besmirched
bewitch
bicycle
billy goat
biographies
biotic
biscuits
bison (plural)
bites
bizarre
boar
boarders
bookshelves
bookworm
bookworms
boot
borders
boring
born
borne
borough
boss

bosses
bough
bought
bouquet
bout
boutique
breath
breathable
breathe
brews
bridal
bride
bridegroom
bridle
briefcase
brigadier
brilliance
brochure
bronchitis
brother
bruise
bruised
build
bull
business
busy

cacti
cactus
cactuses
calendar
calypso
calypsos
campaigning
capable
card
cargoes
cargos
carrier
carrots
carry
cascade
cast
caste
catacombs
catalogue
categories
category
caught
cautious
ceiling
celebration
celebrations
cemetery

centre
century
cereal
certain
chairs
chalet
challenge
chameleon
champagne
chandelier
change
changeable
chaperone
character
characteristic
charade
charismatic
charity
chart
chasm
chauffeur
cheerily
chef
chef's
chemicals
cheque
chic
chided
chief
chiefs
child
children
children's
chisel
chiselling
chivalrous
chivalry
chlorine
chorus
chrysanthemums
circle
city
claim
classifiable
classify
cliffs
climax
clinic
clinician
clockwise
clothes
clout
co-operate
co-operation

co-ordination
co-organisers
coarse
cohere
coherence
coherent
coincide
coining
collaborate
collapse
collapsible
colleagues
collect
collectible
collision
cologne
colour
comely
comet
comfortable
comma
commando
commandoes
commandos
commercial
commission
commit
committee
communicate
communication
communicator
community
compatible
competent
competition
complements
complete
completely
completion
complex
complexes
compliant
compliments
comply
component
comprehend
comprehension
compress
compression
compromising
computers
conceitedness
conceive
concierge

conclusion
conclusive
condor
conduct
confectioneries
confectionery
conference
conferred
conferring
confess
confession
confident
confidential
confuse
confusion
conical
conscience
conscientious
conscious
consequence
consequent
consequential
consider
considerably
considerate
construct
constructable
constructible
consumable
consume
continue
contract
contraction
controversies
controversy
convenience
convenient
convert
cookies
correct
correspond
correspondence
correspondent
cottages
cough
council
counsel
count
counter
counterfeit
countess
courage
course
cow

cower
crescendo
crescendos
crescent
crises
crisis
criticise(s)
crochet
crucial
crypt
cryptic
cryptically
crèche
curiosity
curious
currant
current
cyanide
cyclists

dam
damage
dangerous
daughter
de-emphasise
de-escalate
debatable
debt
decaffeinated
deceivers
decency
decide
decision
decorate
deduce
deducible
deer (plural)
deer (singular)
defenceless
deference
deferral
deferred
defiant
deficiency
definite
delicious
democratic
democratically
demoted
deniable
deny
depend
dependably
dependant

dependence
dependency
dependent
descent
describe
desert (noun)
desert (verb)
desertion
desperate
desperately
dessert
destruct
destructible
detached
determination
determined
develop
developing
development
device
devise
devote
devotion
dictionary
died
differ
differed
difference
different
differing
difficult
diffuse
diffusion
digest
digestion
dignity
diligent
disable
disadvantage
disagree
disagreeable
disagreement
disallow
disappear
disappearance
disappoint
disappointment
disapproval
disapprovingly
disarm
disassemble
disastrous
disbelief
disbelievingly

discard
discolour
discomfort
discontinued
discontinuing
discos
discount
discourage
discourteous
discuss
discussion
disembarked
disenchanted
disgrace
disguise
dishonest
dishonour
dismissal
disobedience
disobedient
disobey
disorderly
disoriented
disown
dispose
dispossess
disqualify
disregard
disregarded
disrespectful
disruption
dissatisfied
dissent
dissimilarity
distilleries
distillery
distort
distortion
distraught
disturbance
divide
divided
divisible
division
docks
doubt
doubts
dough
draft
dragons'
drake
draught
drone
drought

dual
duchess
duck
duel
duke
duller

earl
early
earth
eavesdropper
echo
echoes
echoing
edible
editor
educate
education
eerie
eerily
effect
effective
effervescent
efficiency
eiderdown
eight
eighteenth
eighth
elaborately
elect
election
electric
electrician
eligible
eloquence
embarrass
embarrassment
eminent
emission
emit
emitting
emperor
empress
enchilada
encouragement
endurance
engine
engineer
enjoyable
enough
enviable
environment
environmentally
envy

equestrian
equip
equipment
equipped
erode
erosion
escapade
especial
especially
essential
ewe
exaggerate(d)
excellent
except
exception
exclaim
exclude
exercise
exhaust
exhaustion
existence
expect
expectance
expectancy
expectant
experience
experiment
expertise
explanation
explode
explosion
expose
express
expression
external
extra-curricular
extract
extracurricular
extraordinary
extraterrestrial
extreme

fabulous
facial
fairies'
familiar
famous
farther
fascinated
Fates
favourite
February
feet
fiancé

fiancée
fiasco
fictitious
financial
financier
firemen's
fishes
fit
flames
flimsily
flimsy
flog
flogging
flower
fluorescent
foe
foot
forcible
foreign
forensic
forensically
foreword
forget
forgotten
formal
formatted
fort
forty
forward
forwards
fought
fox
foxes
fraught
freight
frequency
frequent
frequently
fresco
friend
fruit
fuchsia
fund
fungi
furlough
further
fêtes

galactic
gander
garden
gardener
geese
generate

gilt
giraffe
giraffes
girl
girls
glacial
glacier
glamorous
glasses
glue
gnashed
gnomes
god
goddess
gondolier
goose
gorilla
gout
govern
government
grace
gracious
graduate
graduation
grammar
graph
grate
grave
gravely
great
grieved
groom
grotesque
group
guarantee
guarantees
guard
guerrilla
guessed
guest
guidance
guide
guilt
gymkhana
gymnasium
gyroscope

hail
hairs
hale
handkerchief
handkerchiefs
handle
hangars

hangers
harass(ed)
harsh
harshly
hart
hazardous
heading
headmaster
headmistress
heard
heart
height
heir
heiress
hen
herbivorous
herd
hero
heroine
hesitance
hesitancy
hesitant
hesitate
hibiscus
hiccough
hideous
hierarchical
hinder
hindrance
hippopotamuses
his
historic
historically
history
hoard
hoarse
hoarsely
hoaxes
honest
horde
hour
house's
human
humane
humongous
hygiene
hymn
hysteric
hysterical
hysterically

ibis
ibises
idealistic

idealistically
identity
igloo
igloos
ill-advised
illegal
illegible
illegitimate
illiterate
illogical
illustrate
illustration
imaginable
imagine
imbalance
immaterial
immature
immediate
immediately
immigrate
imminent
immobile
immoral
immortal
immoveable
impaired
impartial
impatient
impelled
imperceptible
impersonal
impersonated
impertinent
implant
implausible
implied
impolite
important
imported
imposed
impossible
impractical
imprecise
impress
impression
imprisonment
improbably
improper
improve
imprudence
imprudent
inaccessible
inaccurate
inactive

inadequate
inadmissible
inadvisable
inanimate
inappropriate
inattentive
inaudible
incapable
inclined
include
inclusion
incompatible
incompetence
inconclusive
inconsiderate
inconsistency
inconsistent
incorrect
increase
increment
incur
indefinable
indefinite
independent
indestructible
index
indicate
indication
indices
indignity
indirect
indistinct
individual
induce
inducible
inedible
ineffective
inefficiency
ineligible
inequality
inexperience
inexplicably
infamous
infectious
inference
inferred
influential
infomercials
informal
information
informed
infused
ingredient
inhibit

inhumane
injected
injustice
inner
innocent
innovate
insects
inseparable
insert
insertion
insignificance
insistent
insufficient
insured
insuring
intake
intend
intention
interact
interchange
intercity
interconnect
interest
interested
interfere
intergalactic
interim
interjected
interlaced
interlibrary
intermediate
intermission
intern
international
interpersonal
interplay
interred
interrupt(ed)
intersects
intertwine
intervene
interview
intrude
intrusion
invalid
invent
invention
irrational
irreconcilable
irredeemable
irregular
irrelevance
irrelevant
irreparable

irreplaceable
irresistible
irresponsible
irretrievable
irreverent
irreversible
irritate
irritation
island
isle
isosceles

jab
jabbed
jealous
joyous
judicial
juiciest
justice

knapsack
knave
knaves
knowledge
knowledgeable

label
lad
lady
lamb
lampshade
lampshades
language(s)
laps
lapse
larva
lass
lava
lead (verb)
league
learn
led
leeks
legal
legible
leisure
length
lenience
lenient
lessen
lesson
liabilities
liability
library

lice
licence
license
lieutenant
lightening
lightning
like
likeable
limit
limitation
lions
literal
literally
llamas
loaf
loan
loaves
lone
lord
louse
luscious
luxuries
luxurious
lyric

machete
machine
madam
magic
magically
maidservant
malevolent
malicious
man
manservant
marchioness
marine
market
marquis
martial
martyr
marvellous
mascot
master
matchstick
matchsticks
material
mattress
mattresses
mature
medal
meddle
medicine
men

mention
mentionable
merged
metal
mettle
mice
micro-organism
microbiologist
mine
miniature
miniatures
minute
misaddress
misalign
misapplied
misapprehension
misbehave
miscalculate
mischievous
misconception
misconduct
miscount
misdeed
misdiagnose
misdial
misdirection
miserably
misfire
misfit
misgovern
misgovernment
misguide
mishandle
misheard
misinformation
misjudged
mislabel
mislaid
mislead
misplaced
misprint
misregard
misremember
misremembered
missed
misshaped
mission
misspeak
misspelled
misspelt
mist
mister
mistletoe
mistreatment

mistress
mistrustful
mobile
mobiles
mode
monarchy
monk
monotonous
moose (plural)
moose (singular)
moral
morning
mortal
mosque
mosquito
mosquitoes'
mosquitos'
mountainous
mourning
mouse
moustache
mouths
moveable
mowed
Mr
Mrs
muscle
music
musician
myself

nag
nagging
naive
naively
nanny goat
national
natural
naught
naughty
naval
navel
necessary
negligent
neighbour
neighbourhood
niece
nonsense
nostrils
notice
noticeably
nought
nowt
nuclei

nuisance
nun
nutritious

oases
obedience
obedient
obey
oboes'
obscene
observance
observant
observe
obsess
obsession
occasion
occasionally
occupancy
occupied
occupy
occur
occurrences
occurring
offered
offering
officials
offspring (plural)
offspring (singular)
often
omission
omit
omniscient
opaque
operate
operation
opportunity
opposite
optic
optician
oral
orchestra
orchid
ordinarily
ordinary
ought
ours
ourselves
outrageous
overpopulate
overpopulation
ox
oxen

packed

pact
palatial
parachute
parallel
parliament
partial
particular
passed
past
patience
patient
patients
patriotic
peahen
peal
peculiar
peel
people's
perceptible
perhaps
perilous
permission
permit
persistent
personal
persuadable
persuade
persuasion
persuasive
persuasively
pertinent
phenomena
phenomenon
photosynthesis
physical
physique
pictures
picturesque
piecemeal
pieces
piercingly
pilfered
pilfering
pistachio
plague
planets
plant
plaque
platypus
plausible
plod
plodder
plough
pneumonia

poisonous
polite
pollute
pollution
poltergeist
pompously
popular
pose
position(s)
possess
possession
possible
potatoes
potential
pout
practical
practice
practise
precarious
precede
precious
precipitous
precise
precisely
precocious
predict
prediction
preen
preference
preferred
prejudice
preparations
prepare
prequel
president
presidential
pressure
pretentious
prevent
preventable
prevention
prince
princess
principal
principle
print
privilege
privileges
proactive
probably
probing
proceed
prodigy
profess

profession
professional
proficiency
profit
profiterole
programmable
programme
project
projection
prologue
promise(d)
promote
promotion
pronoun
pronounced
pronunciation
properly
prophecy
prophesy
prophet
prosperous
proudly
prove
provincial
prowler
prudent
psyche
puff
puffs
puppies'
purchase
purpose
pyre

quart
quarter
quarts
quartz
queasy
querulous
query
quest
question
questionable
questions
queue
queued
quiet
quizzes'

racial
racquet
radios'
radishes

ram
rational
re-editing
re-elected
re-employ
re-enter
re-evaluation
re-examining
reacquaint
react
reactive
readily
ready
reallocated
reapplied
reassurance
rebellious
reboot
rebuilt
receipt
receipts
recent
recipes
recipient
reclaim
reclined
recognise
recommend
recommendable
reconcilable
reconnect
reconsider
recur
recurring
redecorate
redeem
redeliver
redesigned
redirect
redoubling
reduce
reedy
reek
refereed
reference
referendum
referral
refill
reformed
refund
refused
regard
regarded
regenerate

regret
regrettable
regular
reign
reimburse
reincarnation
reindeer
reins
rejected
relative
relevant
reliable
relieved
remarkable
remember
remission
renovate
repaired
repelled
repetitious
replaceable
replant
replay
replied
reported
request
reside
residence
residency
resident
residential
resilience
restaurant
retake
reverse
reversible
review
rhetoric
rhetorician
rhinoceros (plural)
rhinoceros (singular)
rhinoceroses
rhyme
rhymes
rhythm
rhythms
ridiculous
rogue
roofs
rooster
rough
route
ruff
rung

rustling
rye

sacrifice
sailor
sallow
scarves
scenery
scent
sceptre
scheme
schemes
scholar
scientific
scimitar
secretary
seized
semiautomatic
semi-automatic
semicircle
semicolon
sensibly
sentence
sentences
separable
separate
separately
septic
sequential
serial
series
shaped
sheep (plural)
sheep (singular)
shepherd
shepherdess
ship
shipping
ships
shoes
shoes'
shoulder
shouldered
signature
sincere
sincerely
sincerity
sir
sire
sister
snakes
social
societies
soldier

soldiers'
solemnly
son
sort
sought
sour
south
sovereign
sow
spacious
special
species
spines
spinster
squeak
squeeze
squelch
stag
stake
stars
stationary
stationery
statistic
statistician
steak
steal
steel
steward
stewardess
stomach
storey
story
straight
strange
strength
strum
strummed
stupendous
sty
subcategories
subcommittee
subconscious
subcontinent
subdivided
subdivision
subeditor
subheading
submarine
submerged
submission
submit
subscript
substance
substantial

subtitle
subtract
subway
success
succession
succumbed
suffered
suffering
suffice
sufficiency
sufficient
suggest
suggestible
suggestion
suite
sultan
sultana
sunburn
sunburned
sunburnt
superb
supercomputers
superficial
superglue
superhuman
superimposed
superman
supermarket
supernatural
supersede
superstars
superstitious
supervision
supposable
suppose
surfer
surfing
surprise
surveillance
survey
susceptible
suspend
suspension
suspicious
swat
sweet
swot
symbol
symptom
syndicate
synonym
system

tangibly

tangos
taught
taut
technique
tedious
teeth
temperature
temporarily
that
theft
their
theirs
therefore
these
they're
thief
thieves
this
thistle
thorough
those
thou
though
thought
throat
through
throughout
thunderous
thwart
tigers
tigress
tiles
tiptoed
title
told
tolerable
tolerance
tolerate
tolled
tom
tomato
tomatoes
tomorrow
tongue
tooth
torpedo
torpedoes
torpedos
tough
tow
tract
transceivers
transfer
transference

transferring
transgress
transgression
transmission
transmit
treacherous
trek
trekked
tremendous
troop
trough
troupe
trout
true
twelfth
twine
tympani
typhoon
typical

unabridged
unacknowledged
unadvertised
unappetising
unbearable
uncharacteristic
uncle
uncompromising
undefinable
under
understandable
undrinkable
unemployment
unfashionable
unfocused
ungrammatical
uninsured
uninterested
uninvited
unique
unit
unofficial
unpatriotic
unperceived
unprofessional
unremarkable
unrepentant
unresolvable
unveiling
urchins
urge
urgency

valid

variable
variety
various
vary
vegetable
vehicle
vehicles
venomous
vicious
vigorous
vixen
volcano
volcanoes
volcanos
voracious
vow

waiter
waitress
waltzes
warlock
wart
wary
way
wear
weary
weather
Wednesday
weight
weird
well-received
were
wet
we're
where
whet
whether
whine
whose
who's
widow
widower
wife
wine
witch
wives
wizard
woe
woman
women
wonderful
wreak
wreck
wrinkled

wrought
wrung

yacht
years
yield
yours (plural)
yours (singular)

zero (singular noun)
zeros (plural noun)